india

india

decoration · interiors · design

Henry Wilson

Watson-Guptill Publications/New York

First published in 2001 in
the United States by
Watson-Guptill Publications,
a division of BPI Communications Inc.,
770 Broadway, New York, NY 10003

First published in 2001 by
Conran Octopus Limited
A part of Octopus Publishing Group
2–4 Heron Quays
London E14 4JP
www.conran-octopus.co.uk

Publishing Director Lorraine Dickey
Commissioning Editor Emma Clegg
Copy Editor Barbara Mellor
Proofreader Barbara Roby
Indexer Peter Barber
American adaptation Josephine Bacon
Creative Director Leslie Harrington
Executive Art Editor Megan Smith
Production Director Zoe Fawcett
Senior Production Controller Manjit Sihra

Library of Congress Control Number: 2001088716
ISBN 0-8230-2513-6

Artwork drawn by Henry Wilson from original
architectural and interior motifs

Printed and bound in Italy

first page Detail of a wood block-printed design
taken from a piece of antique fabric.
previous pages: left New embroidered leather *jutis*
(slippers) hang on the walls of a cobbler's shop.
Ahmedabad, Gujarat.
previous pages: right The interior of a Bohra row-
house in the town of Siddhpur, Gujarat.
opposite Terracotta and brass water-pots in a village
house in Saurashtra district, Gujarat.
front cover Special pieces of appliquéd fabrics and
selected textiles in exuberant, bright colors,
reflecting the magnificent Rabari quilts.
back cover The border of a tribal woman's skirt.

contents

Dehra Dun •

• Delhi

• Mandawa

• Jaipur

RAJASTHAN

Devi Garh
•
Siddhpur • Udaipur
• Ludia •
• Bhuj • Dungarpur

• Ahmedabad
GUJARAT •
Rajpipla

culture & design

Pencil-sharpening and procrastination must be the twin banes of anyone attempting to write anything that endeavors to embrace India in its entirety. It just is not possible. Even the great travel writers have been floored by the extraordinary cornucopia that is India: writers such as Hsüan Tsang from seventh-century China, the Frenchmen Bernier in the seventeenth century and Rousselet in the twentieth, and the Englishmen Colonel Todd, Bishop Heber, and Kipling in the nineteenth century, to name only a few. All have been amazed and exhilarated by the diversity of India, and by its wondrous buildings and the exquisite skills of its painters, decorators, craftsmen, and craftswomen. Not least among these travelers was Mark Twain, who journeyed to India in the late nineteenth century to describe it for a curious audience back home. He soon realized just what a monumental task he had undertaken: "When you think you have come to the end of her tremendous specialties and have finished hanging tags upon her as … the Land of the Plague, the Land of Famine, the Land of Giant Illusions, the Land of Stupendous Mountains, and so forth, another specialty crops up and another tag is required." In the end, he concluded that no less ambitious a title than "Land of Wonders" would suffice.

India's history is so wide-ranging and ancient as to be overwhelming: archeological excavations in Gujarat have revealed evidence of settlements dating back to 3000 B.C.; indeed, India contains the oldest living city in the world, the holy Hindu city of Varanasi. Whereas most of the world's continents can boast one major empire or civilization, India has bred a multitude, including the great Buddhist empire of

Ashoka and the medieval Hindu empire in the south. From the sixteenth century, the great Mughal dynasty reigned from Delhi in the north, before the British arrived to make Calcutta in the east the second city of their world empire. Only since 1947 has India been its own unified master.

All this history and culture are bounded by one of the longest coastlines in the world. Within this natural boundary lies a breathtaking variety of landscapes and habitats, including the world's highest mountains and areas of greatest rainfall; parched deserts and teeming rainforests; great rivers that meander so shallowly to the coast that each year they bring devastating floods; arcadian pockets such as the valley of Kashmir, sitting in the cupped palms of the Himalayas; miles of coastline that produce one of the great staples of life, salt; and fertile lands that grow spices for the world, and which in the sixteenth and seventeenth centuries attracted the attentions of European maritime adventurers like bees to a honey-pot.

Much of India's culture and wealth has been influenced and created by trade, and the subcontinent has for centuries been crisscrossed by trade routes. One of the most famous, still in existence after hundreds of years and now more congested than ever, is the "Grand Trunk Road" which crosses the country from the Pakistan border in the west to Calcutta in the east. Nor were trade routes confined to the land, for India also boasts an ancient tradition of navigation on the high seas, with redoubtable merchant adventurers developing huge fortunes. The togas worn by Roman senators were made from Indian cotton, and scraps of cloth of Indian origin dating from around the

left An assorted collection of posters illustrating various Hindu gods, including Shiva, Krishna, Ganesh, and Hanuman on the wall of the night watchman's room at the Chanwar Palki Walon-Ki *haveli*, Amber, near Jaipur.

7

ninth century have been found in Lower Egypt; much later, some of the battleships for Nelson's Trafalgar fleet were built in India from Indian wood. Not surprisingly, foreign merchants and adventurers yearned to investigate the source of this trade and discover the wealth they presumed it must have created. Thus it was that trade, with its accompanying exposure to the wider world and to other societies and cultures, attracted waves of the inquisitive and the avaricious—including the Mughal, Portuguese, Dutch, French, and British—over hundreds of years.

Such epic comings and goings have left their mark on India, and are most immediately visible in the country's architectural legacy. Lord Curzon, British viceroy from 1898–1905, declared that India possessed "the greatest galaxy of monuments in the world." Today its architecture encompasses an extraordinary variety of forms and styles,

reflecting differences in climate and religion, as well as the legacy of numerous invaders and colonizers. Before these cultural and physical invasions, however, India had already developed its own distinctive styles. Examples of these are evident in the painted caves of Ajanta from the Buddhist period (third to fifth centuries A.D.), or the Hindu southern capital of Vijayanagara (c1350–1565). But so much of India's distinctive architecture owes its unique character to a cross-fertilization of cultures, marrying the Mughal with the Rajput, Muslim concepts with Hindu craftsmanship, Hindu styles with British tastes. The results of this cultural journey now encompass architectural extremes, from the simplest of human habitations, the indigenous roundhouse, to the ultimate in sophistication, elegance, and artistry, as represented by the Mughal Taj Mahal. Perhaps more than any other country, India has absorbed a huge diversity of

opposite A man meditates on his beads, seated on a terrace high above the Ganges River. Varanasi, Uttar Pradesh.

above left A woman stands stoically against the fall dawn chill proffering a *puja* lamp as she awaits the appearance of Lord Surya, the sun god. Varanasi.

above right On the day of the full moon at the end of the Kartik month, crowds converge to bathe at Panchaganga Ghat, Varanasi.

left Akash Deep, the "sky lantern festival." Throughout the fall month of Kartik, wicker lanterns are lit at dusk and dawn to aid the visiting spirits of the dead to find their way to the other world.

above and below left In the urban environment, color and design are to be found wherever you turn your head, whether it be mounds of dye powder, design on the most mundane of domestic packaging, the exterior of giant "All-India" haulage truck cabs,; mudguards on auto-rickshaws, political graffiti, billboards advertising movies, and religious shrines and temples. The urban street is a visual cacophony of advertisements and cloth banners as each shop, large and small, vies for the customers' attention. Color and design touch every part of life in a country in which the visitors' senses are sent reeling, additionally provoked by boundless sounds, odors, and movements.

left A poster painter balances precariously on wooden scaffolding to hand paint a hoarding for a store selling soda pop and wine. Many giant movie theater and advertising billboards are still hand painted by artists. However, technology is gaining a foothold, with computer-generated images and industrial printing now being used.

cultural influences, subtly adapting them to its own needs simultaneously, yet without diluting that inherited sense of a special Indian identity.

The Indian creative canvas, with its constantly shifting cultural nuances, has found expression in every conceivable material, metamorphosing the basic components of stone, wood, mud, iron, and paper into a staggering variety of expressions of human delight and exuberance. Religion has been the catalyst for much of this adventure into decoration, in the form of the Hindu temple, the Muslim mosque, the Buddhist shrine, and the Christian church. Secular influences have also been at work in the art of ornamentation, conspiring to elicit flamboyant acts of collective extravagance from a people who individually have tended to be rather sober and restrained.

Ornamentation finds further expression through color, which in India is used in vivid, kaleidoscopic fashion. Color is applied to virtually every imaginable human creation, from the mundane to the most refined. In the spring festival of Holi, it is even used to celebrate life itself, as Day-Glo pink

powders are flung about with wild, raucous abandon in a huge nationwide celebration. During Diwali, the Festival of Lights, many millions of fireworks explode in iridescent rainbow colors as, not satisfied with coloring the earth, Indians set out to paint the heavens as well. Color is everywhere in India, both physically and metaphysically. Entire towns or cities may be painted a single color, such as the blue of Jodhpur in Rajasthan, an earthly echo of the color of the blue god, Krishna. Saffron is the color of religious asceticism, white of mourning. Color is also used as a form of identification, as in the handsome turbans of Rajasthan. At annual cattle and camel festivals, the many thousands of people who gather from all over western India can deduce from a single glance at the color and pattern of a man's turban not only the district he comes from but even his home village.

One of the greatest and most profound expressions of color in India is to be found in its textiles. Here again, India compounds the difficulties that face anyone attempting an overview of this tradition, with an apparently infinite number of forms, styles, and uses evolved over millennia. Great centers of textile production have sprung up all over India, and some locations have become especially renowned, such as Kashmir for its shawls and southern India for its silks. Gujarat in the northwest is another historic center, producing textiles that were lauded across the world as far back as the fifteenth century. Custom-designed products were made for the various international markets. For instance, the textiles created for the Mughal court in Delhi and the royal families of Thailand, Burma, and China attained the most exquisite heights of refinement and sophistication. European demand was so great that Italian, French, and British adventurers established thriving trading houses in Gujarat in order to satisfy the requirements of their aristocratic clients. So delicate were Indian muslins that when laid on the grass at dawn they might be mistaken for dew, and some shawls were so fine that they could be drawn through a ring taken from a slender finger. Today Varanasi is renowned for its hand-woven Benares silk brocades, Jaipur is famed for its handmade block-printed fabrics, and the district of Kutch in Gujarat is noted for its exquisite embroideries.

Alongside the textile trade, there developed many other artistic and creative crafts, including carpet-weaving, wood-carving, brasswork, stone-carving, and pottery. Carved wood was used all over India, but most particularly in Gujarat and Ahmedabad, where it was worked with exquisite intricacy and applied to the great merchants' houses, known as *havelis*. In this city, with its almost equal populations of Hindus and Muslims, craftsmen from both communities vied with each other in the craftsmanship and artistry of their designs, producing wonderfully intricate examples of wood-carving. Elevated standards were also attained in the marble masonry work inlaid with precious stones that was perfected in Agra, and which is displayed not only in the magnificent Taj Mahal, but also in the small, perfectly proportioned tomb of Itmad-ud-Dualah. Nothing short of sublime, this monument is encrusted with a decorative inlay of carnelian, jasper, lapis lazuli, malachite, and other stones, while the designs of the façade echo the beautiful garden that surrounds it. Virtuoso

masons transformed great sheets of white marble into the fine fretwork of *jalis* (pierced screens), which create dream-like patterns of dappled light within the enclosed verandas.

The crafts of India are the creation of generations of families, who over the centuries have honed their particular art to remarkable heights of refinement. Typically, a son was introduced to his father's speciality from a young age, in due course taking over the bulk of the work and the responsibility for supporting family and parents. Retirement was the signal for the older generation to start work on their magnum opus, a labor of many years which, when finished, was worthy of the gods themselves.

It is these craftspeople who are the heroes and heroines of India's creative heart. They, more than anyone, have created the look of India today, through a myriad of architectural masterpieces and fine works of art. And they have made not only the monumental but also the domestic and practical. *India* surveys this extraordinary abundance of creativity as seen in the Indian home and its interiors, designs, and decorations. It focuses on one particular area of the subcontinent, stretching from the Arabian Sea to a point in the low foothills of the Himalayas and taking in Gujarat, Rajasthan, and Delhi. It is a route that provides a wealth of breathtaking imagery, from the graceful halls of Samode to the stunning façades of the grand mansions of Shekhavati, and from the tribal roundhouses of Kutch to the sophistication of a contemporary Delhi residence.

These pages are an invitation to cross the threshold of the Indian house and discover in it an extraordinary variety of design and decoration. As some of these images may inspire readers to adapt them for their own homes, line drawings have also been included; these may be turned into traced stencil plates and then combined with the inspiring colors of the country, so bringing something of Indian style to other homes on other continents.

Rudyard Kipling described the Taj Mahal as the "Ivory gate through which all dreams pass." The same may be true of any home, however grand or humble. Shown here is the diversity and exuberance of the Indian interior, a constantly evolving synthesis of India past and present.

Walk down any street, lane, or alley in the old quarter of a city or town and magic doors open onto small rooms of industrious artistic creativity.

above left An artist puts the finishing touches to a painted marble statue of the god Hanuman. Varanasi, Uttar Pradesh.

above right A textile artist from the Vaghari community applies dye to a cloth painting with a religious theme. Ahmedabad, Gujarat.

below A man stretches out sari fabric that has just been tie-dyed. Bhuj, Kutch, Gujarat.

merchant houses

| bohras of siddhpur | wooden havelis of ahmedabad |
| frescoes of shekhavati |

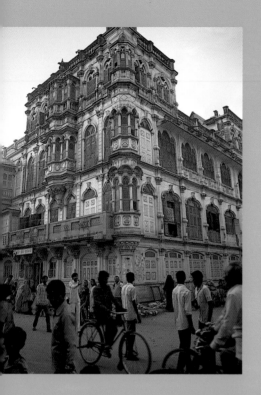

above left A grand Bohra *manzil* (mansion) on the Broadway of Siddhpur in Gujarat reflects the commercial flair of the Bohra community.

above right A group of retired Bohra elders congregate for morning coffee.

line drawing on page 14 Detail from a relief design found on the front of a terraced Bohra house in Siddhpur.

opposite Detail of the refined wood-carving found in the Bohra houses.

For hundreds of years, India has been a great trading nation. Its merchant class has a long and successful pedigree, particularly in Rajasthan and Gujarat. Much of India's contact with the outside world has been through trade, and this is reflected in the houses of the merchant class.

Three groups of merchants, in particular, have incorporated differing and distinctive features into their houses. The Bohra *manzil*s of Siddhpur are laid out formally along broad avenues, constructed and decorated in European style; the Shekhavati *haveli*s are justly famed for their frescoes; and the *haveli*s of Ahmedabad are renowned for their remarkable decorative wood carvings. Driven by a spirit of rivalry among themselves, with each group anxious to inhabit the biggest and best *haveli*s, their owners were consistently generous patrons of the arts and crafts, who engendered a quality and diversity of creativity that will probably never be achieved again.

The town of Siddhpur is located in northern Gujarat, in a bucolic setting of tranquil fields filled with lemon-yellow mustard flowers. Located several hours' journey from the nearest big city, how could Siddhpur possibly be anything other than a small and parochial rural settlement? Yet from the shadow of its great Edwardian-style clock tower, the

view down Siddhpur's impressively wide main street is more reminiscent of the metropolitan grandeur of Mumbai (Bombay) or—by a stretch of the imagination—Paris. The boulevard is lined with elegant and imposing four- and five-story *manzil*s, also in an unabashed early-twentieth-century British style, while regiments of row houses in the same manner line avenues leading off on each side.

The town dates from the tenth century, yet the Bohras are relative newcomers, having arrived from Ahmedabad in the early twentieth century. Originally of the high caste of Hindu Brahmins, whose rigid precepts precluded any involvement in business dealings, they converted to the Muslim faith and took to commerce with zest. Loosely translated, the name Bohra means "one who is true to the ethical principles of business."

The Bohras thrived under British rule as the railroads came to Gujarat, expanding their businesses across India and beyond to the Far East and Africa. In the early years of the twentieth century, the Bohra council in Siddhpur decided that the old town was too congested and bought a plot of barren land on the outskirts of the town to build a "new" township, which still appears incongruous in its native surroundings. More than any other merchant

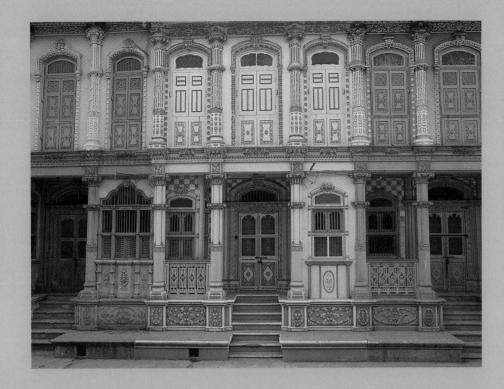

community, the Bohras were heavily influenced by British urban styles of the period, not only in the architecture they favored, but also in the layout, decoration, and furnishings of their own homes.

The façades of their houses were considered the ideal place for a proud display of wealth and success. Embellished with baroque and Art Deco designs, and painted in cotton-candy colors, they indicate nothing of the Muslim culture of the inhabitants. Each house frontage included a plaque bearing the family monogram, usually positioned beside the front door, applied in relief and picked out in color, following a European tradition imported by the British. The entwined initials of the family were combined with those of the city in which they had established their businesses, and in some cases, the families also adopted the name of that city, so creating titles such as Calcuttawalla and Adenwalla.

Each house is entered across a raised threshold with a small sitting area in front of the main door, while the front room is shielded from public view by an Edwardian-style screen set with glass panels that are hand painted with landscapes of the Ponte Vecchio or Mount Fuji, copied from postcards with some license by local artists. Inside, the full

extent of foreign influence becomes clear. Gone is the traditional open courtyard, in favor of a narrow air shaft for ventilation. The traditional mud floor has been replaced with tiles, smart and easy to maintain, laid in repeating geometric patterns, and dados painted with local scenes have been replaced with European-style decorative tiles. Guests are entertained formally in the drawing room in back of the building, where mattresses covered with white sheets and lavish Persian-style rugs mark a return to tradition. Built-in closets in Burmese teak double as storage space and display cabinets, their elaborate carving frequently crowned with extravagant crests, again echoing the European aristocratic grand tradition.

The merchant houses of Ahmedabad differ from those of Siddhpur and Shekhavati in a number of respects, and not least in their setting. The origins of the former capital of Gujarat stretch back as far as the eleventh century, and the old walled city is congested and compact. In contrast to the freestanding mansions of the Marwaris or the rigorous grid pattern of the Bohra "new town," the Ahmedabad *haveli*s seem buried in a labyrinth of lanes and alleys. In former centuries, Ahmedabad was a thriving production center for many commodities, including weapons, and, above all,

above left The Bohra terraced houses are notable for their consistent architectural structure. The surface decoration, however, presents a mixture of styles, the most popular being Art Deco.

above right A Bohra mother and daughter prepare to go shopping. The women, though Muslim, are not obliged to cover their faces in public, unlike in some Indian communities.

above left The main
courtyard of the Manganbhai
haveli in the old quarter
of Ahmedabad in Gujarat.
above right Whether
substantial or small, every
Ahmedabad *haveli* has carved
ornamentation on the
wooden frontage.

textiles. The city's climate made it ideal for cotton spinning and weaving, so that when the British arrived, it became a focus for industrialization. At its peak, it boasted over fifty cotton mills, each employing some four to five thousand workers. Many grand *haveli*s were built from the profits of this trade, but inevitably, the mill owners began to forsake the crowded old city for new mansions that incorporated all the latest comforts and conveniences. As a consequence, many of their old homes in the walled city were left deserted.

Although neglected for so many years, the buildings remain intact, thanks to their method of construction. While the houses of Siddhpur and Shekhavati were primarily of stone, the Ahmedabad mansions were built half of brick and half of wood, the dry climate that favored cotton also favoring timber production. When local supplies ran out, wood was imported from the Malabar Coast of southern India and from as far away as Burma.

The *haveli*s are frequently raised above street level, with verandas running the width of the frontage. Above the veranda is a cantilevered upper floor, further supported by either an elegantly proportioned wooden arcade set in stone, or by beautifully carved struts. Skilled wood-block

cutters from the textile industry probably also worked on the *haveli*s. The carved woodwork of the façades is certainly as fine as that required for block prints. Artisans from both the Hindu and the Muslim communities worked on these mansions in a spirit of intense rivalry, their different styles and subject matter leading to tremendous diversity in their work. The deeply carved supporting struts of the upper stories are exquisitely worked with mythical creatures and flowing floral motifs. On the upper floors, architraves and rafters are a riot of intricate design, including flowers, leaves, creepers, carved elephants, peacocks, and the cheeky, emerald-green parrots that are virtually an unofficial emblem of India.

The mansions of the Shekhavati district in northern Rajasthan belong to the families of the Marwari business community who today hold center stage in the rapidly expanding economy of modern India. Initially, they made their fortunes from the trade caravans that crisscrossed the region on the way to and from Delhi, south to the Arabian Sea and on to Africa, west to present-day Pakistan and on to Iran, and north to Kabul in Afghanistan and thence to China. Later, the British arrived in the guise of the East India Company, and land-based trade routes withered as the

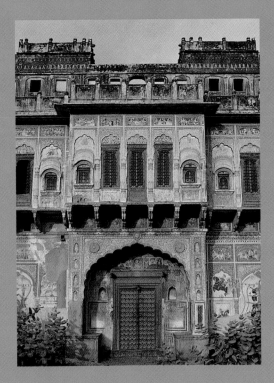

colonialists established the great seaports of Calcutta and Bombay. The shrewd Marwaris moved to the new ports, and particularly to Calcutta, where they now form the single biggest, wealthiest, and most influential section of the population. Under the British, they became agents, brokers, and financiers in the seaports, specializing in commodities such as opium, tea, jute, silver, and gold. A portion of the fabulous wealth accrued by the Marwari merchants was sent back home, where it was used to finance the building of magnificent *havelis*.

In the late nineteenth century, a feverish passion for new building gripped the Marwaris, in tandem with a craze for fresco painting, all provoked by the heady spirit of one-upmanship that now consumed the merchants. Fresco painting is a traditional skill in Rajasthan, and as the new buildings went up, local artists were offered large, fresh canvases to work on. Each *haveli* had to be bigger and better and each fresco brighter and more delicately painted than the next. Every local artist was dragooned into service, reinforcements were brought in from all over the state as well as from neighboring states, and the wealthiest merchants lured the most talented court painters to come and work on their mansions.

In such a competitive climate, the owners were not particularly concerned with the subject matter of the paintings, and therefore gave the artists free rein. Their chief artistic inspiration came from religion, but they also depicted kings and queens and their courts, everyday scenes of women drawing water, hunting scenes, floral and geometric motifs, and portraits of animals such as elephants and camels. The subject matter also reflected the changing times. Through the seaports, the Marwari merchants were exposed to the world beyond India, and more particularly to the wonders of the Industrial Revolution. On their annual visits to their desert mansions, they brought back lithographs and drawings of marvels such as steam trains and ships, horse-drawn landaus, and Mr. Ford's new four-wheeled contraption, which were duly included—in delightfully incongruous fashion—in the frescoes on their walls. The chemical reaction between the water-based pigments and the lime plaster of the walls has lent the frescoes a surprising degree of permanence despite the glaring sunlight of the location. Because the pigment was applied to the damp plaster, the artists had to work very fast before the plaster dried, creating a distinctively fluid and spontaneous style.

above left A night watchman sits guarding a *haveli* in the Shekhavati district.
above center Many of the grand fresco-decorated *havelis* in the Shekhavati district have been abandoned, as their owners are now living in the big cities.
above right The *haveli* entrances have elegant cusped arches and are furnished with heavy, solid doors.

bohras of siddhpur

The Bohras of Siddhpur created a new business empire for themselves in the early twentieth century. One result of this was a magnificent new town in Gujarat. One of the avenues running off the central mall clearly shows the somewhat incongruous influence of British metropolitan style, as filtered through the Raj. Bohra dwellings were influenced by European tastes in both their design and their decoration, as may be seen in the furniture and intricate plasterwork.

opposite The new quarter alongside the old town of Siddhpur was strikingly constructed on a grid pattern with long, orderly streets. It presents an incongruous sight in Gujarat, with its broad sidewalks and uniformity of façades.

left Many of the frontages of the Bohra row houses were wholly influenced by the Art Deco style. So enthusiastic were the Bohras about the prevailing fashion, that the façades are devoid of any indication of the ethnicity of the owners.

opposite One of the most distinctive features of a Bohra front room is the *hitchkar*. This swinging seat comes in many styles, depending on the period when it was made. This example is seen in its basic functional form of a slab of wood with a mattress and brass rods, although *hitchkars* often have highly decorated seats, with wood carvings and inset tiles.

above Carved wooden screens were inset with sandblasted or acid-etched glass. This ceiling is decorated with fine plasterwork in a European style. The magnificent carved wooden balustrade adds a formality and grandeur that also owes much to European influence. The floor is covered with mass-produced tiles in geometric patterns.

left The focal point of a Bohra house is the place where the drinking water is kept. The first thing a guest is offered on a visit to a Gujarati household is a glass of water. Water is stored in *mutka*s, terracotta pots that sweat in the high ambient temperature. This evaporation keeps the water deliciously cool. Water is raised to the point of sanctity and is often stored in what looks like a shrine.

right A detail of the intricate plasterwork ceiling. Picking out the plasterwork in color was a matter of taste and was not done in every case.

below A detail taken from the plaster relief bordering the main ceiling.

right The Bohra householder was not afraid to use color, representing the arrival of the Industrial Revolution, when new synthetic, permanent, and industrially made pigments became available. The Bohras, whose business took them far away and overseas, would have been exposed to the new fashion for color. The mass-produced metal-framed bed, introduced by the British, soon began to replace the traditional wood-framed, string-bottomed charpoy.

left Bulbous European-style swags in plasterwork hang from the cornice, while ornate wood-framed mirrors with decorative crowns dominate the walls. The European influence is evident throughout, from the 1950s period fabric on the sofas to the Aubusson-style rug.

below The formal drawing room is on the first floor in back of the house. It shows a partial return to tradition in the mode of seating with pillows lined up against the walls. The expensive Indian rug is generally covered with calico to protect it from dust and sunlight.

far left and below The plaster-decorated ceilings are a distinctive feature of the Bohra interior. Like the Marwaris in Shekhavati, the Bohras were traders in the great Indian seaports but also went much further afield. One Bohra reached such heights of wealth and influence in the court of Emperor Haile Selassie in Addis Ababa, Ethiopia, that he became known as the "Uncrowned King of Ethiopia."

above right This mirror-fronted door decorated with fruit, birds, and flowers has a distinct feel of the Ottoman Empire.

opposite The Taj Mahal is justly a source of great pride in a Muslim household. Madraswalla is the family name, adopted from Madras, the city in which their business thrived.

wooden havelis of ahmedabad

It was said that Ahmedabad hung on three threads—gold, silver, and cotton. The earliest of the city's wooden *haveli*s date from the fifteenth century, and for many years these were the homes of the city's rich merchants, who created immense wealth. The most profitable of their numerous business activities were based on cotton, textiles, and particularly the indigo dye for which the city was famous. The exquisite mansions still stand, hidden in the labyrinth of the old city, their flamboyant displays of fine wood-carving surviving as an outward sign of the status, grandeur, and good taste of their erstwhile owners.

left The main courtyard of a *haveli*. A tissue-paper kite hangs from the rooftop. Kite flying and kite fighting are popular pastimes, particularly in January when the festival of Uttran takes place.

below left It might be assumed that these grand mansions, buried deep in the heart of the old city, would be suffocatingly hot in summer, but the worst of the heat is kept at bay with cross-ventilation, ventilation shafts, deep courtyards, and the *hitchkar*.

below right All the interaction with the outside world took place in the first courtyard of the *haveli*, entered directly from the street. This is where the very best of the wood-carved façades would be positioned, letting any visitor know that the merchant was wealthy and successful.

opposite and left The façade of the merchant's *haveli* that faced the street was reserved for the finest of the decorative wood-carving. The city had a tradition of carving through its position as a center for textiles, whose fabric printing demanded the highest standard of craftsmanship in the carving of wood blocks. This skill could be adapted for the decoration of the *haveli*s. There was energetic competitiveness between the merchants and the craftsmen themselves to have the most florid and exquisitely carved façades. These are details from the carved wood-panel façade of one of the grand merchants' *haveli*s.

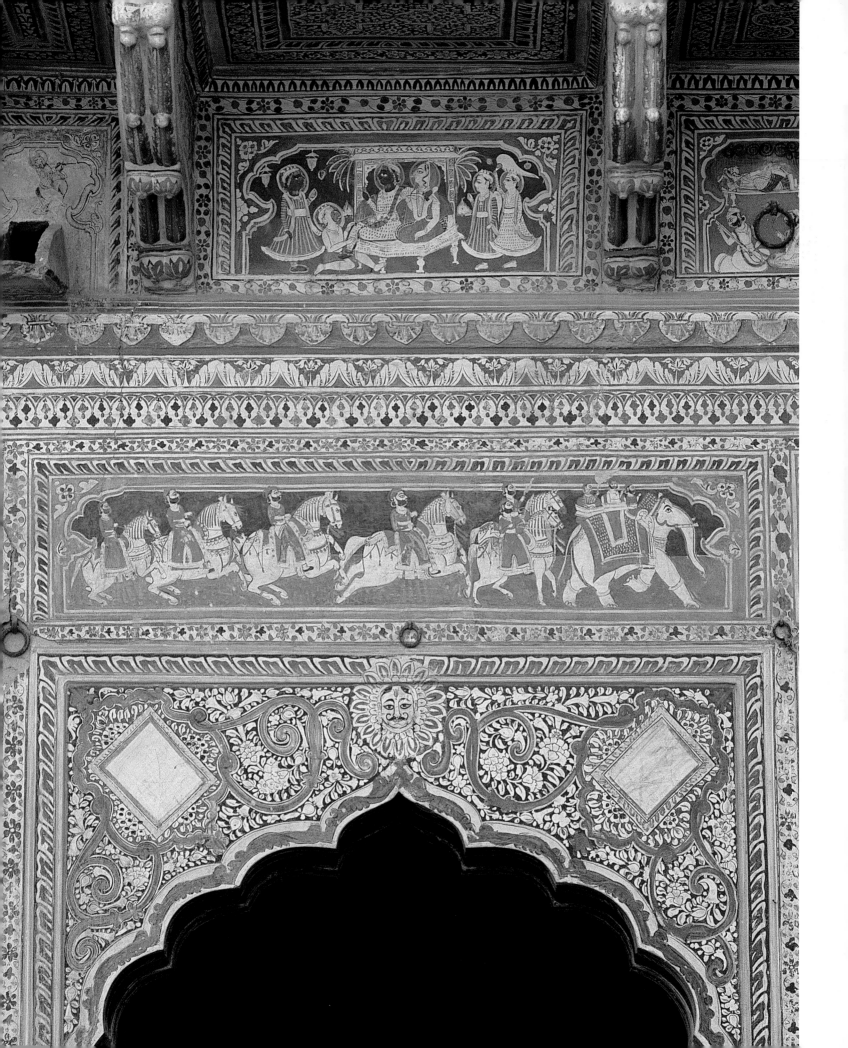

frescoes of shekhavati

The painted façades of the handsome and imposing *havelis* that make up the desert towns of the Shekhavati district of northern Rajasthan are unmistakable. Built for Marwari merchants as impressive displays of their wealth, they are painted inside and out with a remarkable gallery of frescoes on religious, royal, and everyday themes. Nowhere else in India, or indeed the world, boasts such prolific amounts of fresco work. The colorful decoration forms a strong contrast with the drab surroundings of scrub desert, where temperatures soar to fifty degrees centigrade in summer and plummet below zero in winter.

उड़नेवाला जहाज़

previous pages: left The flat, smooth finish of the grand stone mansions of Shekhavati was a perfect surface on which to paint on rather than carve.

previous pages: right A single *haveli* accommodated an extended family consisting of three generations, along with various family branches. Rivalry gripped the merchant families who competed with one another to have the biggest and most exuberantly frescoed building.

left and opposite The *haveli* frescoes were painted over a period of three hundred years, and richly illustrate social change and developments in lifestyle, particularly during the nineteenth century. There was a fascination for the products of the Industrial Revolution, such as the steamboat and steam locomotive, the automobile, and the Wright brothers' first airplane. Alongside these quirky images were subjects that were more familiar to the owners, such as *shikar*s (tiger hunts), Royal Durbars, portraits of princes, and religious themes.

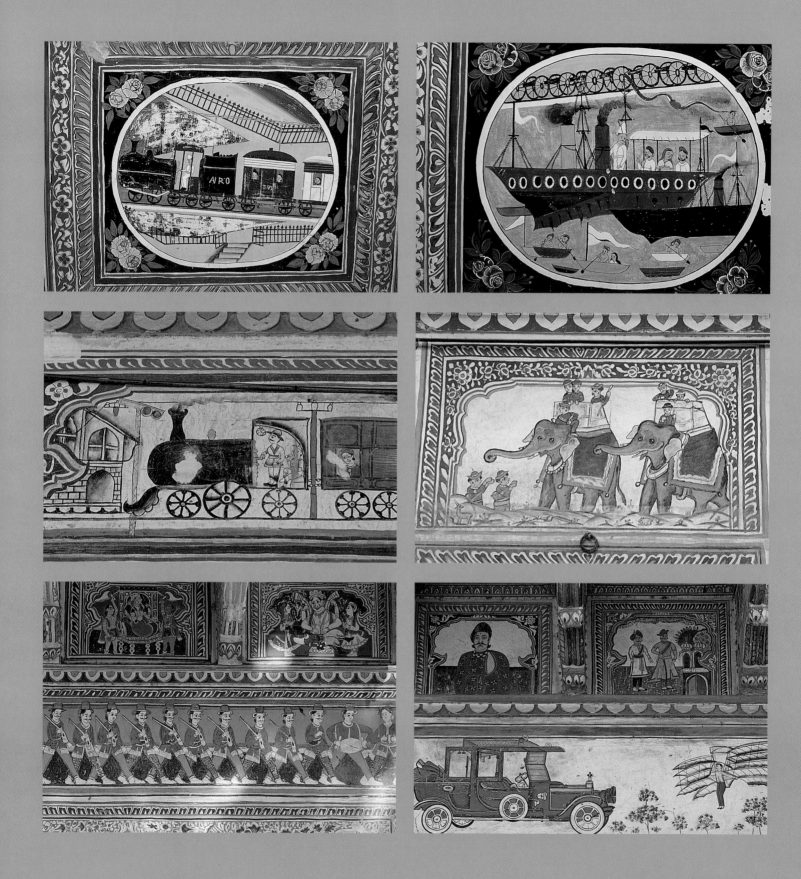

left The finest frescos were reserved for the interior, and the richer the merchant, the better the artists he could afford. No surface was left untouched, including the awkwardly shaped ceilings. Producing a fresco involves creating a chemical reaction between the water-based pigment and lime plaster. Painting had to be completed quickly while the plaster was still wet, resulting in a free-style form of illustration.

opposite The entrance to a merchant's *haveli*, where some of the finest frescoes are found. This one shows *ferengi* (foreigners), *topi wallas* (hat men) and their *barra sahibs* (foreign ladies) with their crinolines and parasols, a popular subject.

below Border detail from a painted *haveli* of Shekhavati.

left Not only did merchants build extravagant homes, but they paid for buildings and facilities for the wider community. They believed that this would guarantee them a place in heaven so did not stint on the quality. Temples and shrines were as exquisitely painted as their own houses, with religious scenes and illustrations of Indian mythology as is illustrated in the interior of the dome of a temple.
below An example of the exuberance of the fresco painters of the nineteenth century, this ceiling has been covered with geometric and floral motifs. The band of portraits consist of rosy-cheeked, white-faced ladies and gentlemen in refined clothes. All of the characters wear hats, these being strongly associated with these foreigners.

forts & palaces

| samode palace | neemrana fort | udai bilas palace | devi garh fort |

above left Samode Palace rests at the end of a valley in the Aravalli hills outside Jaipur. The imposing façade symbolized the ruler's power.

above center Samode Bagh is a garden paradise recently restored by the current family, about a mile from the palace.

above right Dancers of the Kabalia caste perform for guests in the exquisitely decorated durbar hall of the palace.

artwork on page 42 Detail of the cut-glass mosaic work in the Udai Bilas Palace, Dungarpur.

opposite Detail of the painted walls of the hall behind the Sultan Mahal, Samode Palace.

As recently as fifteen years ago, the royal palaces of India appeared doomed. It seemed that four hundred years of glory, despotism, wealth, intrigue, loyalty, and service had finally come to an end. These magnificent structures had become millstones around the necks of the families whose ancestors had built and defended them, and their very fabric was crumbling as they became home to monkeys and bats. But as tourism grew, many owners shed their shyness of business in the cause of preserving this unique architecture. The greatest concentration of forts and palaces is to be found in the state of Rajasthan, where they were built by the warrior clan of Rajputs, the Kshatriya caste. Samode Palace near Jaipur, Neemrana near Delhi, and Udai Bilas and Devi Garh, both close to Udaipur, are four Rajasthani palaces that once seemed certain to vanish forever. They have been saved by returning to their fine tradition of hospitality, receiving guests once more, but now in return for payment.

For centuries, Rajasthan and its maharajas have exercised a fascination over foreign imaginations, inspiring stories of rivers of blood, of women throwing themselves on the funeral pyres of their husbands rather than submit to enemy capture, of wild excess and generosity, of intrigue and betrayal, of codes of honor, devotion, and loyalty, of sybaritic pleasure and extravagant piety. The maharajahs of Rajasthan were all this and more. Two hundred years ago, only a handful of foreigners were able to witness a few glimpses of this extraordinary and mysterious world. Richly embellished descriptions of an earthly paradise traveled back to the West, and the fascination of the world of the maharajahs continues to draw visitors today.

The geology of Rajasthan is the oldest in the world, making for a wild and forbidding landscape. Even a century ago, travel was arduous, slow, and in high summer almost unbearable. After days of discomfort on dangerous roads, the sudden view of one of these fortified palaces must have been wondrous. More often than not they cling to the side of a boulder-strewn hillside, monumental fortified citadels with sheer walls crowned by crenellated battlements and embellished with clusters of *chattris* (domed pavilions) and *jharokas* (decorated covered balconies). Not unlike the great cathedrals of medieval Europe, these Rajput palaces had the effect of instilling awe and respect in those who surveyed them, their sheer bulk and height indicating the power and authority of an absolute ruler.

The arrival of visitors was never unexpected. Days beforehand, the maharajah would be informed, either by guards posted along the way or by heliograph (mirror

telegraph) of imminent arrivals. Visitors of sufficiently elevated status would be granted an audience with the potentate in the durbar hall, the main public reception room. The full durbar protocol afforded the most effective occasion for the maharajah to display the regal pomp and ceremony that emphasized his power. Tales of such audiences describe the maharajah seated on an elevated *gaddi* (throne) beneath a gold-embroidered and bejeweled velvet parasol, looking down upon his royal household and a multitude of aristocrats. Smoldering braziers filled the durbar hall with a mist of aromatic incense, and palace retainers sprinkled the assembled audience with headily perfumed rosewater. Foreign visitors were both thrilled and overawed, not only by the assembled royalty but also by the decorative splendor of the durbar halls.

Samode Palace is not only one of the most exquisite creations of the period but also one of the finest of all the Rajput palaces, and its breathtaking durbar hall lives up to every expectation. Of particular brilliance are its painted walls and ceilings, created under Rawal Berisal Singh in the mid-nineteenth century. The Sultan Mahal is an exquisite example of the Jaipur miniature style at its best, with every inch meticulously painted with geometric and floral motifs; the dados represent garden borders filled with flowers and

mango trees and inhabited by a profusion of every species of bird found in the region. The rulers of this desert state loved gardens, and this hall brings the delights of an imaginary garden indoors.

In the 1970s, there seemed little future for Samode, as for so many other palaces, but then its two youthful heirs, Rawal Raghavendra Singh and his brother Rawal Yadavendra Singh, took on the task of saving the property, and opened it to a discerning public. Slowly, with considerable thought, sensitivity, and integrity, they have returned the huge palace to its former splendor, rightly assuring it a place of honor among India's heritage hotels.

To the northeast of Samode lies the hill of Neemrana. A fifteenth-century, fortified palace perches on a natural plateau midway up the steep slopes. After Independence, it became impossible to maintain such large structures. In 1946, an entire wing collapsed, and in the 1950s the heirs could not maintain what was left. The deterioration continued for another twenty-five years, until Aman Nath and Francis Wacziarg stumbled across the ruin and, with two other like-minded people, bought it.

The palace complex had been vandalized and all its architectural details pilfered, rooms lay open to the sky, and floors had subsided. The new owners wanted to turn it into

above left Neemrana Fort, viewed from the village below. Both a royal home and a fortress, its high position and strong ramparts reflect the importance of its defensive role.
above right A stone soldier in a cusped arch marks a staircase that leads up to the main body of the fort.

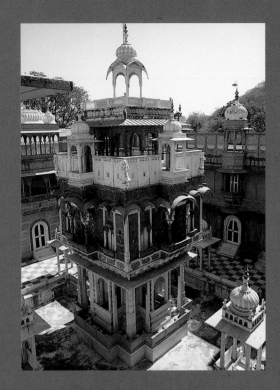

above left A pavilion rises out of the main courtyard of Udai Bilas Palace, Dungarpur. Built in the Indo-Saracenic style, it was once linked by a bridge to the main building. **above right** The palace looks out over Lake Gaibsagar, an important resting-place for migratory birds in winter.

a hotel, but first had to clean up the rubble and shore up the walls before even beginning the rebuilding work. Passionately interested in India's architectural and craft heritage, Nath and Wacziarg have become spirited protagonists of a growing movement to rescue what is left of India's heritage, or as Nath puts it, "saving historical architecture picked from the national garbage can."

Today, Neemrana encapsulates Nath and Wacziarg's design ethos, innovative in spirit and monastic in ambience. As inveterate hunters of antique furniture and custom-made accessories, the new owners are keen to encourage traditional craftsmanship. Each room is equipped with unique pieces of furniture and elegant hand block-printed fabrics. Aman chose the colonial style, explaining that "it has the whimsy of the Indian craftsmen in their interpretation of the European originals. The native workmen rarely knew when to stop."

The early twentieth century saw a flurry of palace building by the maharajahs. Indian princes were frequent travelers to America and Europe, visiting the great aristocratic houses of Britain and France and finding inspiration in an eclectic mixture of styles, from French château to Art Deco. Other edifices, such as the Udai Bilas Palace on the shores of Lake Gaibsagar at Dungarpur, some

two and a half hours' drive south of Udaipur, adopted the Indo-Saracenic style, a distinctive fusion of British and Indian architectural elements.

Built in the late nineteenth century in a single wing along the lakeside, the palace was modernized and extended on three sides in the 1940s to form the present courtyard plan. All the interiors were newly decorated in a style that was transitional between the Edwardian and Art Deco styles, yet there was also room for pure Rajput decoration in the form of painted glass panels and exquisite glass inlay, among the finest to be found in Rajasthan. All the rooms are filled with Edwardian and Art Deco furniture and fixtures, and papered with 1940s floral wallpapers imported from London. The maharajah at that time, Udai Singh II, was an enthusiastic convert to the European lifestyle, and the magical Juna Mahal (old palace) was vacated for the new building, which had every modern convenience, including piped hot and cold water, electricity, and above all, space. Western-style bathrooms boasted smart enamel bathtubs and huge cauliflower showerheads. The concept of the dressing room was also incorporated to accommodate the fashion for European dress, and the durbar hall was replaced by an English-style drawing room with Edwardian armchairs and sofas upholstered in 1940s fabrics.

Harshvardan Singh, the present Maharaj-Kumar of Dungarpur, has given up a hectic business and social life in Delhi and Mumbai for the tranquility of Dungarpur and the company of his two labrador dogs. Determined to preserve this excellent example of Indo-Saracenic and Art Deco style, he has shrewdly opened the palace to paying guests while also preserving its distinctive ambience. Maintaining the impression that the palace is still a private residence, he invariably invites his guests for a genial early evening drink in the great drawing room.

Forty-five minutes northeast of Udaipur is the small town of Delwara, overlooked by the classic Rajput fortified palace of Devi Garh, the latest addition to the growing number of fine palace hotels in Rajasthan, whose story is similar to that of Neemrana. Deserted by its ancestral owners, it was vandalized and stripped of everything of value decades ago and abandoned to its fate. In 1984, Lekha Poddar and her son Anupam came across the site, and so there began an ambitious project to restore the skeleton of the palace to its original state in every detail. Local craftsmen and traditional techniques were used wherever possible, along with local materials such as Udaipur stone and marble. Restoration, reconstruction, and preservation were the key words throughout the project.

Similarities with Neemrana or indeed any other fort project ended at this point, as the equipping, decorating, and furnishing of the palace took a dramatically different turn. The Poddars were determined to create a maharajah's palace to suit the twenty-first century. As a result, Devi Garh is audacious and visionary. Lekha Poddar and the Mumbai-based interior designer Rajeev Saini have created an interior that fuses the past, present, and future in a combination of the Indian spirit with a rigorous international minimalism.

White and green local marble have been used throughout. A point was made of using traditional methods to create clean, contemporary lines and unadorned surfaces. Each room is themed with a different semi-precious stone, such as malachite, cornelian, jasper, lapis lazuli, or mother-of-pearl.

India has always been open to ideas beyond its borders, seemingly unhampered by the fear of losing its own identity, and Devi Garh is an outstanding example of this broad-minded liberalism. The palace finally opened its great spiked wooden gates on the eve of the year 2000. A majestic celebration of India's past, it also stands as a convincing welcome to the twenty-first century and to India's future.

above left The fortified palace of Devi Garh. Once a beacon of civilization in the wild Aravalli hills, it has now been restored with style by Lekha and Anupam Poddar. **above right** A view from a rooftop contrasts the bright limewashed stone of the palace with the rocky hills beyond.

samode palace

Samode Palace, about thirty miles from Jaipur, represents a distinctive period in the evolution of the fortified palace in Rajasthan. The arrival of the British brought a degree of stability to the region, and with this the need for fortifications receded; consequently, the royal purse was free to indulge in courtly decoration and display. The formal reception rooms, especially the durbar hall and Sheesh Mahal (mirrored hall), are masterpieces of painting and glasswork, featuring intricate geometric designs and an explosion of flowers, birds, and figurative motifs.

left The grand durbar hall is the formal reception area of the palace, where in the past the Rawal of Samode would have received royal visitors, dignitaries, and senior British administrators. Few other interiors can rival the skill of execution and the ravishing beauty of the decoration.
opposite The ceiling in the durbar hall is hand painted and features geometric and floral patterns alongside portraits of nautch girls (professional dancers).
below Detail of the border below the open shuttered window in the durbar hall.

left The elaborate painted decoration shows no expense was spared in the adornment of the various public rooms of the palace. The arrival of the British secured greater stability in Rajasthan, so that where previously money would have been spent on waging war or on defense, the palace exchequer was able instead to use funds for patronage of the arts.

opposite In the hall behind the Sultan Mahal, every surface has been painted. The ceiling has swirling floral motifs in a Dutch blue; the dado is decorated with pencil firs, mango trees, and various species of garden birds; landscapes include detailed illustrations of sites of religious pilgrimage.

below Detail of paintwork on the cornice of the Sultan Mahal.

above The Sheesh Mahal runs alongside the durbar hall on the upper level. The entire ceiling and upper walls are covered with convex pieces of mirrored glass. What would have been a dark space has become delightfully bright, the myriad pieces of mirror playing with reflected and rereflected light. The Sheesh Mahal also had a more romantic purpose. The Rajput men at one time spent much of their lives outdoors, hunting or protecting their families. Their lives changed in the 1900s as they settled down to more sedentary pursuits, spending more time at home rather than outside. Lighting candles under the mirrorwork in the Sheesh Mahal would create just the effect of the celestial canopy under which they used to camp.

below left The Sultan Mahal is a public reception area for intimate gatherings. The silver furniture, sofas, *charpoys*, and footstools were brought from Nepal; the dhurries and rugs were all locally woven in Jaipur. The walls are painted with flowers, bowls of fruit, and scenes from religious mythology.

below right The ceiling and upper portions of the decorative *jharoka* in the Sultan Mahal have been covered in mirrored glass and overlaid with delicate gesso tracery work. Not only is the jharoka a decorative focal point; it also practical, letting in light along the back of the Mahal.

artwork Detail of a floral design taken from the dado rail in the Sultan Mahal.

above This small anteroom overlooking the durbar hall that is finished in monochrome provides a clever contrast to the ravishing paintwork of the durbar hall, seen through the archway. The women of the palace would have used this room and the corridors running around the sides of the hall on its upper level as a place from which to view the ceremonies and court proceedings below.

right Detail from a dado running between the Durbar Hall and the Sheesh Mahal; a riot of color, flowers, and birds. In this desert region, gardens were highly prized. The elaborate "paradise gardens" brought color, scent, and birdlife to the rugged surroundings. Great efforts were made to locate sources of running water to supply fountains, ponds, and artificial watercourses, the likes of which can be seen at Samode Bagh.

left An adaptation of a floral pattern from a pierced stone screen.

opposite and above left Gallery along the upper level of the durbar hall. The elegant proportions of the receding arches, enhanced by the curved ceilings, create an impressive passageway. On one side there are views of the palace gardens and surrounding hills and on the other, the gallery overlooks the central hall.

above right The mirror glass patterns in the gallery alongside the Sheesh Mahal are based on a tradition that originated in Iran. Glass balls were blown and mercury poured into them while they were still hot. The balls were then smashed and the shards shaped to fit the design. This gallery and the adjoining Sheesh Mahal are among the finest examples of such glasswork in Rajasthan.

neemrana fort

A fortified palace situated near the highway between Delhi and Jaipur, Neemrana was neglected throughout most of the twentieth century and eventually reduced to ruins. With at least two-thirds of it collapsed, bringing it back to life was a huge task which would have daunted even the most enthusiastic of owners. Through the dedication and determination of Aman Nath and Francis Wacziarg, however, the royal complex was recreated room by room, just like an intricate jigsaw. Together, Nath and Wacziarg combed the country to bring together a fine collection of indigenous and colonial furniture, which has now been installed in surroundings that are elegant, tranquil, and monastic in atmosphere.

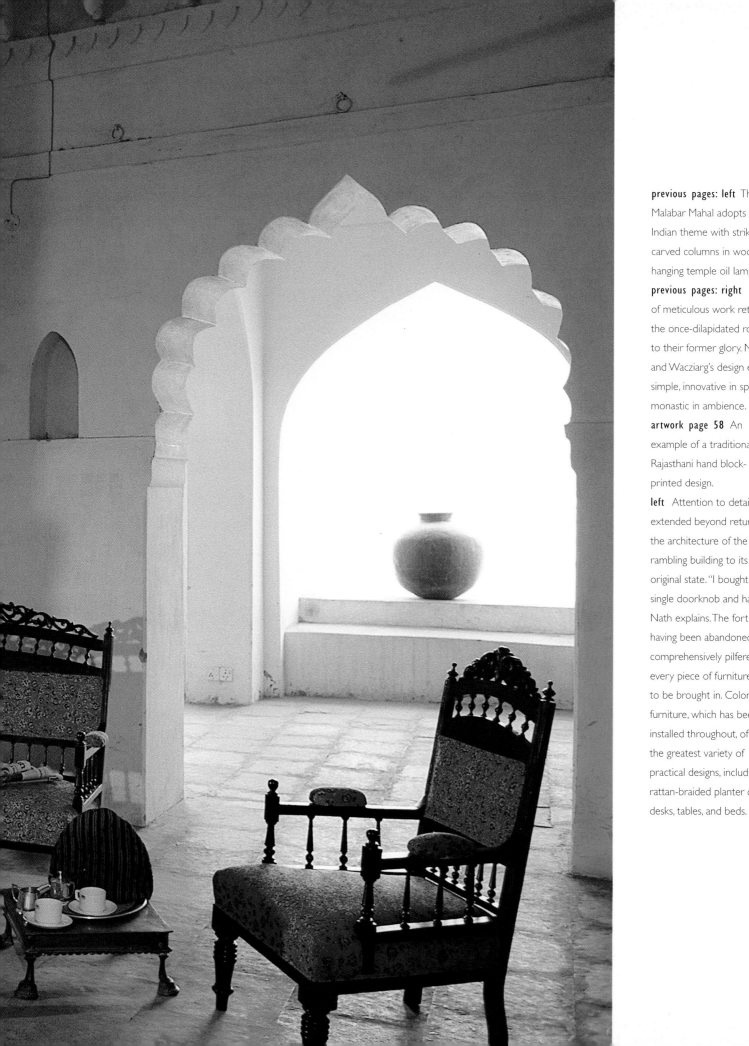

previous pages: **left** The Malabar Mahal adopts a south Indian theme with striking carved columns in wood, and hanging temple oil lamps.

previous pages: **right** Years of meticulous work returned the once-dilapidated rooms to their former glory. Nath and Wacziarg's design ethos is simple, innovative in spirit, and monastic in ambience.

artwork page 58 An example of a traditional Rajasthani hand block-printed design.

left Attention to detail extended beyond returning the architecture of the rambling building to its original state. "I bought every single doorknob and handle," Nath explains. The fort having been abandoned and comprehensively pilfered, every piece of furniture had to be brought in. Colonial furniture, which has been installed throughout, offers the greatest variety of practical designs, including rattan-braided planter chairs, desks, tables, and beds.

61

left and below Not all the rooms are grand; some are small and intimate. Because the fortified palace stands on an elevated position on a hillside, there are magnificent views across farmland. Few windows are glazed, so light mosquito mesh fills the space and the natural flow of air around the hill passes through the numerous doors and windows. The wooden window shutter flap doubles as a writing desk.

opposite A natty traveling washstand from the colonial period. After use, the basin is drained and folded away. The small water tank positioned behind a mirror would have been kept filled by household staff, but is now plumbed in permanently.

udai bilas palace

The Udai Bilas Palace on the lake at Dungarpur was first conceived as an informal weekend retreat from the large thirteenth-century palace of the Juna Mahal above the town. The original building, constructed in the late nineteenth century, was extended with three new wings between 1940 and 1944 to take its current form. The decoration is an extraordinary fusion of Indian and European style, with British floral wallpapers and Art Deco furniture forming a contrast with the traditional decorative mirrorwork and stained glass. With one of the finest collections of hunting trophies to be found anywhere in the world, it is a beautifully preserved memorial to royal India on the eve of Independence.

opposite One of the most dramatic departures from the traditional interior was the use of mass-produced wallpapers, imported into India in the early part of the twentieth century. The English country flowers at first appear incongruous in a Rajput palace, yet they do reflect the Indian love of flora and fauna, also shown in the carpeting. Only the pictures of Rajput princes and the white marble temple on the lake suggest that the room is an Indian one.

left The crystal glass standard lamp in the grand entrance hall was imported from Europe.

below The trophies in the first-floor lobby are examples of many throughout the palace. In the early twentieth century, the Maharajah frequently sailed away to East Africa on safari, later flying out for shoots in Kenya and Tanzania.

right The painted decoration of flora and fauna has the effect of bringing the outside gardens inside the palace. The colored mica panes admit light while also softening it. The intricacy of the glasswork on the decorative panels belies the difficulty of working the material. The fragile glass is awkward to handle and each piece must be cut with a diamond-tipped stylus.

opposite One of the main bedrooms of the palace. This is an example of the fusion of Western period furniture, Art Deco, and Rajput interior decoration. The covered porch overlooking Lake Gaibsagar is decorated with Rajasthani painted glass and mirrorwork of the finest quality, which gives this riot of flora, fauna, and birds a jewel-like quality. The floor of the adjoining vestibule, seen through the door, is covered in large tiles of mirrored glass. Western influences are found in the plasterwork of the ceiling, the cornice, and the way in which the wall space has been divided. The cabinet houses the radiogram and was also used as a bar.

opposite Detail taken from the colored glass mosaic of the covered balcony overlooking the lake.

left Four details of the painted glass, mirror, and mother-of-pearl patterns that are to be found on walls and columns around the palace. Flowers predominate along with parakeets, wild boar, crocodiles, insects, tortoises and fish.

opposite The lotus flower is considered a symbol of divinity and purity, a perfect bloom that rises clean out of the muddy waters, reaching up to the sun. "In the beginning were the waters, matter readied itself. The sun glowed and a lotus slowly opened, holding the universe on its gilded pericarp." (Indian creation myth).

devi garh fort

The remodeling of the fifteenth-century fortified palace of Devi Garh is one of the most audacious projects in India today. Devi Garh has been transformed into a visionary minimalist hotel. Lekha Poddar and her son Anupam, working with interior designer Rajeev Saini, have deftly combined the Indian spirit with cutting-edge contemporary design. Minimalism has been tempered with the judicious use of color, as in the custom-designed Benares silk brocades and semi-precious stones such as lapis lazuli, malachite, and jasper. The restyling of the interior abandons historical reconstruction in favor of an imaginative projection of a maharajah's palace for the twenty-first century.

opposite The main public reception room had been subjected to decades of neglect, and was pillaged when the building was abandoned. Once the fabric of the building had been rejuvenated, it was remodeled to suit a twenty-first century, forward-looking prince. The lotus pattern, hand woven in Benares, is a contemporary example of the ancient art of brocade weaving.

left Wherever possible, architectural features were preserved, including the cusped arch (top left), the column and corbels, and statue and *jharoka* in the dining area (bottom right). The contemporary table settings (bottom left) complement the period surroundings. An installation (top right) is dedicated to the great Lord Shiva, with an antique wood carved head of Shiva and a series of brass tridents, part of Lord Shiva's sacred implements.

artwork Detail of a repeat lotus design chiseled into the stone balustrade in one of the courtyards.

left The seamless, clean lines of the marble bed base, low coffee table, shallow flower dish and flower vase are distinctive.

right Each of the bedroom suites has consistent design features, all the surfaces and accessories being finished in white. Then, a single jewel-like color is introduced, saffron in the case of the honeymoon room shown here. The shower of marigolds and mango leaves traditionally forms the canopy beneath which the sacred rights of the Hindu wedding are performed.

below left A floor detail in one of the suites. Sandstone has been exquisitely inlaid with green marble and mother-of-pearl, using the lotus design theme that pervades the palace.

below right Detail of a wall in one of the garden suites, on which the design of a mango tree in bloom has been carved out of the thick white marble in relief. All of the rooms have been kept spartan, enabling what decoration there is to stand out dramatically.

opposite The convex mosaic glass-filled niche is a traditional decorative feature that is given a contemporary look when set within entirely plain surroundings. The white marble vases were commissioned for the hotel and carved by local craftsmen. Their simple lines are uncluttered by ornamentation.

opposite artwork Detail of the lotus design used on the silk brocade panels in the durbar hall.

opposite An old royal elephant seat (*howdah*) with glass inlay and delicate relief work hints at how the palace was decorated before it fell into ruin.

left The classically styled chairs are skillfully covered with hand-beaten metal sheeting, in a style contrary to the traditional embellishing of surfaces with pattern.

below The Mumbai-based interior designer Rajeev Saini has worked to produce a fusion between the spirit of India and cutting-edge contemporary design. The synthesis of original architectural detail, particularly the gray stone columns that surround this room, and the use of gray-and-silver contemporary chairs, is particularly harmonious. Numerous marble bowls were commissioned for the complex, and here, two elegantly cusped examples are filled with water, then sprinkled with pale pink blossom; another example of the auspicious use of color within a scheme dominated by monochrome.

opposite artwork A representation of the sun god Lord Surya, from the *howdah* above.

tribal

| traditional huts | modern bhungas |

above left Muslim Jat tribal women collect water from a local well to take back to their homes.

above center Terracotta is still widely used for the storage of grain and water.

above right A young Rabari girl is dressed up in preparation for a religious celebration.

artwork on page 78 Detail from the piece of Rabari embroidery on page 86.

opposite Detail of the wood-carving on the shutters of the contemporary bhungas near Ahmedabad, Gujarat.

Even after fifty years of rapid industrialization and urbanization, India remains a rural society. There are areas scattered across the subcontinent that are still inhabited by poor tribal populations, generally uneducated and living on the fringes of society. Although Indian culture has been continually exposed to foreign influences through successive centuries, these tribal groups have tenaciously resisted them. Three groups of tribal homelands are shown here, all in the state of Gujarat in western India. The Rabari and Meghwal tribal groups of Kutch live in western Gujarat, a desert region close to the border with Pakistan, while the Rathva tribal peoples are in eastern Gujarat, in the hill district of Panchmahal. The Rabari are nomadic and pastoral, moving to wherever grasses are available for their sheep, camels, and goats. The Meghwal have settled down to a degree; they still herd sheep and goats, but now derive their main income from leatherwork. The Rathva are farmers and forest hunters. The Rabari and Meghwal are Hindu, while the Rathva are animists. These contrasts between environments and religious practises have directly influenced the style and decoration of their homes.

The Rabari and Meghwal live in distinctive *bhunga*s (roundhouses), consisting of cylindrical, adobe walls topped with a cone of thatch, and supported by a single central post.

Such structures date back to the earliest forms of human habitation, as attested by the delight of archeologists on finding evidence of a post-hole dating from thousands of years ago. Like other types of Indian tribal construction, there is no kind of formal architectural input, the builders being the homesteaders themselves, who collect their materials in the immediate vicinity and use only natural resources such as mud, sticks, and giant grasses. The Rathva live in a hilly, forested environment on the other side of Gujarat, very different from the Rabari lands. Their rectangular huts are made of bamboo and mud, with roofs of adobe tiles.

These contrasting styles of tribal architecture have developed to suit the differing local climates, so that each type of dwelling is able to exist within its environment rather than challenge it. The structure of the low roundhouses of desert Kutch relies on the inherent strength of the cone shape to resist the force of the constant summer winds. The lack of rainfall—a mere eight inches each year—makes it practical to use mud and thatch, materials that help to insulate the buildings against the extremes of summer heat and winter cold. Structural strength is not a priority for Rathva houses, however, as they are sheltered by forests, which protect them from high winds. Rain is the hostile element here, so adobe roof tiles are used instead of grass.

All three styles of tribal dwelling use adobe, including adobe bricks. Mud is plentiful, malleable when wet and strong when dry, particularly when mixed with straw and cow dung. It is an easy-to-use, cheap, renewable resource. But adobe is now losing out to the growing popularity of concrete, a material with neither the properties of mud nor its esthetic qualities. Sadly, the concrete box is increasingly seen as a status symbol among rural people, more desirable than "inferior" traditional houses, so that many of the old techniques are disappearing. These changes would surely have troubled Mahatma Gandhi, who visualized independent India as a collection of villages across the subcontinent, each self-supporting with regard to food and inherited building skills. But as the tribal people, the principal repositories of adobe technology, turn their backs on their centuries-old expertise, many contemporary Indian architects and designers are waking up to and exploring the magic that is adobe, thatch, and wood. It is ironic that the element of urban culture that has been responsible for the gradual dilution of tribal building and decorative traditions should be the very one that is now helping to ensure their survival.

One architectural team currently exploring this dying heritage is that of Nimish Patel and Parul Zaveri, who are based in Ahmedabad. Having spent years exploring and experimenting with India's building traditions, they have become passionate advocates of the appropriateness of adobe for contemporary building and interior design. Putting their theories into practice, they have created new *bhunga*s for a wealthy industrialist and his family seeking a weekend retreat suitable for meditation and contemplation. Built near Ahmedabad with the aid of craftsmen and craftswomen imported from Kutch, the result proves that adobe and thatch are still practical and are the most esthetic materials in this environment. Faithfully following the interior layout of an original hut would have been too restricting, and a few concessions had to be made to the clients' understandable desire for a degree of comfort. Some of the huts are thus linked by a thatched walkway, tiles are used in the kitchen and bathrooms, and larger windows are let into the walls to increase the level of natural light and ventilation.

These new-style *bhunga*s create the effect of a peaceful rural setting, far removed from the modern urban world. The interiors are a celebration of the rich combination of crafts and textures that is so distinctive to Kutch. They also illustrate just how relevant the traditional approach can be to the contemporary world, both in design and in lifestyle.

above left and right This set of new *bhunga*s built outside Ahmedabad follow closely the materials and structural traditions of Kutch dwellings.

traditional huts

The tribal people of Gujarat are remote from urban life, and even from the rural life of most of their neighbors. Their dwellings are diverse in construction and decoration, reflecting widely differing environments and beliefs. Three examples of such tribal dwellings are illustrated here. The *bhunga*s (roundhouses) of the Rabari in Tunda Wandh on the Gujarat coast in Kutch have been developed to cope with the hot desert climate, using only local materials in their construction, while the interiors are distinctive for their adobe and mirrorwork. The Meghwal dwellings, also in Kutch, are similar in construction. The interiors are also heavily decorated, but even the exteriors feature bold geometric patterns, reinvented annually during preparations for the celebrations of Diwali, the Festival of Lights. In contrast to the Rabari and Meghwal, the Rathva tribes of Panchmahal have rectangular dwellings adorned with energetic and colorful wall paintings that illustrate the "Myth of Creation" and the marriage of Pithoro, the deity who protects the household from the vicissitudes of daily life.

opposite Many of the tribal groups in Gujarat live in *bhungas* (roundhouses). Traditionally, they were made of mud, but concrete is now becoming popular, and here it is the main structural material. The woman of the house embroiders a blouse in the light of the doorway, often the single source of natural light into the roundhouse.

above left The Rathva tribes live in the Chota Udepur district of eastern Gujarat. Their environment is forest and jungle, entirely different from the Rabari and Meghwal who live in the desert of Kutch, Western Gujarat. The Rathva live by hunting and gathering from the forest, harvesting fruits and edible roots. Here, a huge grain storage basket is being woven.

below left A Meghwali woman separates the chaff from the wheat in preparation for the evening meal. While the Rabari finish the exteriors of their homes with whitewash, the Meghwal paint the outsides with bold, naïve geometric patterns that are often symbolic. These same designs are frequently used in their embroidered and appliquéd textiles.

above left A young Rabari boy leaves the plain white-washed roundhouses of Tunda Wandh to tend his sheep.

below left Beautifully embroidered quilts incorporating mirror glasswork, created by the Rabari women, are neatly piled on top of the cabinets.

right The distinctive mud and mirror work of the Rabari, here decorating the storage cabinets around the walls, are charged with symbolic meaning, warning of evil spirits or celebrating gods. The interiors are kept immaculately swept and the floor is frequently given a fresh layer of mud, particularly at festival times.

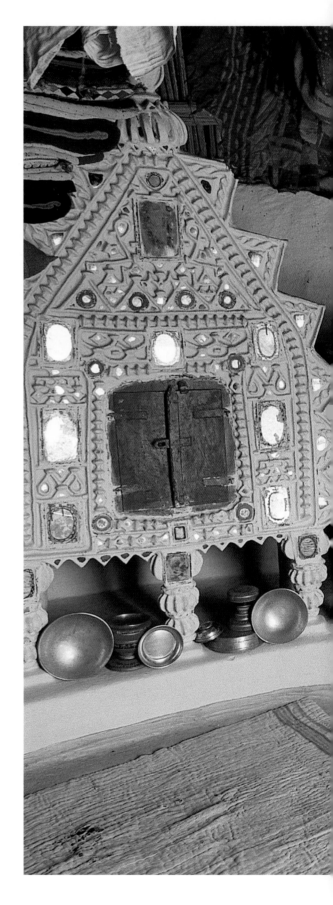

left Detail of a camel saddlebag.

right Detail of a small Rabari shoulder bag. The design is energetic, providing a colorful rendition of a festival, with dancing women and a caparisoned elephant.

opposite The border of a tribal woman's *gagra* (skirt). Quilts, dresses, blouses, and sack-shaped purses all form part of the young girl's dowry, and she and her mother and sisters will have embroidered many of the pieces. The embroidery, adobe, and glasswork traditions are handed down through the generations.

below A detail drawn from the small shoulder bag above.

left The enclosed veranda of the Rathva house is colored with naïve murals illustrating the "Myth of Creation" and the marriage procession of the god Pithoro, the tribe's agricultural deity. Alongside the procession are the tribe's ancestors, events from the living world, animals of the forest, and ghosts. These illustrations have an energy and clarity similar to those of ancient cave paintings.

above A large storage basket for grain and a carved column in a Rathva hut. The horses in the mural are a central theme in Rathva mythology, originating from a time when horse sacrifices were performed.

next page: left The high-maintenance mud floor has been replaced by a dyed cement finish that is snake- and scorpion-proof. The design is based on traditional tribal geometrics.

next page: right The roof of the *bhunga* is thatched, laid on a base of bamboo. Iron bars are installed in the windows instead of glass for security.

next page: artwork Detail of traditional geometric tribal designs taken from the wooden shutters of the hut.

following page Detail of a niche: printed illustrations of Hindu gods and a saint stand alongside incense sticks.

modern bhungas

Nimish Patel and Parul Zaveri have applied their mantra of "simplicity and authenticity" to a set of modern *bhunga*s built as a country retreat for a client in Ahmedabad. The use of adobe and other natural materials of traditional construction has ensured the continuity of the old esthetic sensibility and expertise. As with the homesteaders of Kutch, all the building materials were gleaned locally. Tribal artists were brought from Kutch to create the wonderfully decorative adobe-and-mirror relief work. Parul commissioned special pieces of appliqué fabrics and selected textiles in exuberant, bright colors in order to echo the magnificent Rabari quilts.

left The relief work in the main living area is a combination of flower-based abstracts and geometric patterns. The low storage closet has a bamboo frame around which the mud-and-dung mixture is applied. The lights are known as *arti* lamps, consisting of tiny terracotta dishes filled with ghee, with wicks of hand-rolled cotton.
opposite top left Detail of the mud-and-cow-dung relief finish with inset pieces of mirror glass on the walls.
opposite top right and bottom left Special pieces of appliquéd fabrics and selected textiles were commissioned in exuberant, bright colors to reflect the magnificent Rabari quilts.
opposite bottom right Detail of the mosaic-tile splashback in the kitchen, the design of which echoes tribal patterns.
artwork Detail from the mud-and-cow-dung relief work in a modern *bhunga*.

revival

| amber haveli | pratima haveli | raj bungalow | dehra dun |

above left Chanwar Palki Walon-Ki *haveli* is built into the town wall of Amber, outside Jaipur.

above center Traditionally block-printed quilts are hung out to air in the winter sun.

above right The architectural details of arches and niches are echoed as painted reliefs.

previous page Detail of the hallway in a Raj bungalow, New Delhi.

artwork on page 94 Detail from one of the wood-carved façades of a *haveli* in Ahmedabad.

Crumbling ruins are a common sight in India. To Western sensibilities, such decay and disintegration can be shocking, indicating an apparent disregard for the country's heritage and culture; but this preoccupation with preservation is principally a recent Western concept. The Indian preference is to build new homes to reflect the achievements and success of contemporary generations, rather than live in the shadow of former ages. This attitude among contemporary Indians offers a partial explanation for the decline of classic, older Indian buildings. Old buildings have frequently provided a source of materials for new ones, but today's owners usually live in reduced circumstances compared with their ancestors, and properties suffer from inevitable neglect as family feuds over inheritance—an all-too-common Indian preoccupation—drag on for decades.

While many Indians still consider that progress necessarily implies the rejection of anything connected with the past, a growing and prosperous middle class has introduced an increasing awareness that the country's architectural and design heritage must not only be preserved but also revived. The projects shown here demonstrate a few of the directions that this spirit of revival has taken. Nimish Patel and Parul Zaveri of the

architectural practice Abhikram, along with John and Faith Singh of Anokhi (the hand block-printing company), have come to appreciate the genius of the builders of the past, whose work was so well suited to the land and the volatile climate. John and Kinnari Panikar, meanwhile, have pursued a personal crusade to save as many as possible of the traditional wooden *haveli*s in the old city of Ahmedabad. Inside the home, an increasing interest in ephemera of the past is evident in the collections of Bikram Grewal, which include antique Indian objects from enamelware to four-poster beds and botanical lithographs, while India's rich design heritage is being reinterpreted by top Delhi interior decorator and designer Raseel Gujral Ansal.

The great fortified palace of Amber, built to guard a strategic valley in the Aravalli hills, was abandoned in the early eighteenth century, when Maharajah Sawai Jai Singh decided to build the new city of Jaipur. The busy town of Amber that had served the needs of the citadel went into decline, and today its handsome *haveli*s are fast crumbling away or lie in ruins. It was here that John and Faith Singh bought the Chanwar Palki Walon-Ki haveli, then little more than a shell, during the quest for an old building on which to demonstrate the belief they shared with Patel and Zaveri

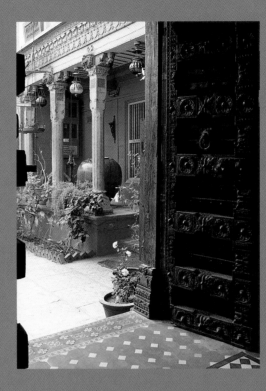

that traditional techniques and materials are still a practical option for today. Having bought the *haveli,* he worked on the project with Nimish Patel and Parul Zaveri. It was Zaveri who first came across the building,

Determined to prove that continuity with the past did not mean stagnation, and that the revival of these old properties was a realistic proposition, they laid down strict parameters. They would use traditional materials and technologies and local builders and craftsmen, who would be fully involved in all decisions. The result is a handsome testament to the original owner's skill in combining taste with practicality, and an architectural and visual triumph. When work began on the restoration of the dilapidated property, fifty workers had to be employed over a period of several years to recreate the structure. As John Singh ruefully recalls, "I don't think anyone builds using local materials and traditional techniques except damn fools like us." His determination to see the plan through has set the standard for other restoration projects.

High walls shade the courtyards from the midday sun, and the dusky blue-green columns—stucco plastered with a traditional mixture known as *aaraish,* created by soaking *kali* (crushed seashells) with yogurt and crystallized sugar in

earthenware pots for a year—remain cool and as smooth as fine marble. Internal and external decoration echo the architecture in a series of shallow reliefs suggesting cusped archways and decorative wall plaques, interspersed with decorative niches that would have been held household objects such as lamps and porcelain bowls or vases. Corbels and cornices have delicate floral motifs painted over the terracotta wash now traditional to Jaipur that has earned it the name "Pink City."

The half-timbered Pratima *haveli* is one of many such historic buildings in the old quarter of Ahmedabad. Kinnari Panikar's family has lived here continuously since it was built nearly four centuries ago, and when she and her husband, John, decided to buy it, they had to negotiate with four quarreling uncles, who met their plans to live in this "run-down, no-go area" with consternation and derision. There had been a general move away from the polluted, dirty Old City and, as if to prove the point, the *haveli* itself had deteriorated into an appalling state. It now consisted of a depressing series of poky partitioned spaces, the floors covered in tired linoleum, and walls painted in gaudy high-gloss colors, all lit throughout by the acid-green glow of fluorescent strip lighting.

above left The inner courtyard of Pratima *haveli* has recently been restored.
above center A view of the front of Pratima *haveli* showing the carved wooden columns and façade.
above right A small courtyard within the *haveli.*

above left A detail of the colonnaded veranda of a Lutyens-style Raj bungalow in New Delhi.
above right The fireplace of the guest bedroom lends a distinctive Edwardian feel to the room.

As soon as John and Kinnari Panikar got their hands on the property, their next task was to set about dismantling the years of ugly additions, scouring the city's architectural salvage yards and antique outlets for appropriate furniture and even original features that had been sold off over the years. Layers of paint were stripped from the teak that had originally been brought all the way from Thailand, while nineteenth-century Italian tiles, the traditional floor covering, replaced the linoleum. The traditional dried-mud finish was restored in appropriate rooms such as the bedroom, where it appears divinely incongruous against the *trompe-l'oeil* painted ceiling.

So many *haveli*s are under threat from property developers that the Panikars have led a campaign to slow down, if not stop, the wholesale destruction of the historic area. In their determination to save what is left, they have put themselves at very real personal risk by frustrating and enraging the powerful property developers. The Panikars offer living proof that the inner city need be neither dirty nor polluted, and in the process have given many of its inhabitants the faith and confidence to tackle more of its restoration. The future looks a great deal more optimistic, owing to their personal example.

Dehra Dun, in the foothills of the Himalayas, provides a perfect antidote to the teeming metropolis of Delhi, a six-hour drive to the south, down on the intemperate plain. Here, Bikram Grewal has adopted another approach to the spirit of revival through his interest in period furniture, textiles, and decoration.

By his own admission, there is nothing remarkable about the structure of this 1970s house, purchased several years ago. Even in its short lifetime, the house had still been allowed to fall into disrepair, so when Bikram Grewal took it over, he had a great deal of work to do to make it habitable. Apart from straightforward repairs, he also enlarged the windows, added a bathroom, and enclosed a narrow veranda that is now known as the "sulking room"! The comfortable and congenial interior, however, has a very strongly defined character, reflecting the climate up in the hills, where in winter the temperature regularly drops below zero. Such a wealth of fabrics, furniture, and floor rugs would be out of place in the dusty, hot plains, but is eminently suitable here.

An avid collector with a particular love of colonial furniture, Bikram Grewal is an inveterate trawler of antique shops; he also attends auctions in Calcutta and embassy

sales in Delhi, while further afield the antique market in London's Portobello Road is a favorite. Grewal has several fine four-poster beds showing the British influence of the Raj. Botanical paintings, drawings, and lithographs from the latter years of the British Raj cover the walls, complemented by the fabrics, which in turn echo the lushly planted garden. A mural in the master bedroom continues this natural imagery while also disguising a set of built-in closets, creating an overall effect not unlike the hand-painted Chinese wallpapers found in British country houses.

This British-style informality finds a striking contrast in the regal manner of a colonial bungalow in New Delhi, with high vaulted ceilings and deep colonnaded verandas, originally built as temporary accommodation for civil servants of the British administration. The present owner, a member of one of India's royal families, wanted it redecorated to provide an appropriate setting for an exquisite collection of *zardozi* work (gold- and silver-embroidered velvets), family silver, portraits, and furniture, and to this end called in the distinguished Delhi interior designer and decorator Raseel Gujral Ansal. Sympathetic to the period detail of the house and its contents, she decided to decorate it in a manner that echoed the sumptuous,

princely residences of the nineteenth century, while at the same time retaining the atmosphere of a home rather than a museum.

The main rooms were designed with high ceilings and low windows to keep out the heat, and consequently have little natural light. In summer, these rooms offer a welcome relief from the May-to-June furnace—cool, shaded and, above all, intimate. No attempt has been made to over-illuminate them. The drawing room, in particular, is a cavernous space, tempered by luxurious thick friezes of stencil work at the top of the high walls and on the ceiling, to designs inspired by the rich ornamentation at Sikandra, near Agra. The effect of this is to enhance the feeling that the space is not unlike a beautiful jewel box. A deep veranda takes on the air of a very large room, especially when the rolls of *chics* (split bamboo roller shades) are lowered. Here Raseel Gujral Ansal has chosen a combination of modern Indian metalwork and Edwardian wrought-iron furniture, covering the walls with broad alternate stripes of white and a dark-golden sand color, which recalls the Indian tradition of sprinkling water on the ground at dusk to damp down the heat of the day, also evoking a unique and delicious aroma of rainwater on parched soil.

above left and right Bikram Grewal's house in Dehra Dun in the foothills of the Himalayas. Running the full length of the building, this veranda provides an alfresco dining area at one end and informal seating at the other.

left A colonnaded arcade faces onto the first courtyard of the *haveli*. High ceilings and the adjacent deep and shaded courtyard provide ample protection from the harsh light and intense heat of the Rajasthani summer.

right A niche at the end of the arcade has been converted into a shrine by the *chowkidar* (watchman), displaying modern images of various Hindu gods and saints.

opposite Where there is no practical need for niches, the walls have been painted with imitations. The entire *haveli* is painted in a particular shade of pink used throughout Jaipur and which has given it the nickname of the "Pink City."

artwork Pattern taken from the decorative niches in the *haveli*.

amber haveli

Painted in the distinctive pink associated with the royal capital of Jaipur, a few miles away, the meticulously restored Chanwar Palki Walon-Ki *haveli* in the small town of Amber stands out amid the ruins of other similar buildings. With the owners John and Faith Singh, along with architects Nimish Patel and Parul Zaveri, a master craftsman and local builders worked for several years to revive this fine three-hundred-year-old building. With its cool courtyards, distinctive archways, and traditional finishes, it is currently an excellent example of how the past can be revived successfully for present-day use.

previous pages: left A view of the first courtyard; this would have been used to receive guests, conduct ceremonies, and for business discussions with the outside world.

previous pages: right The decorated niches served various practical purposes. They held lamps, condiment jars, and betel-nut boxes, or were used to display decorative objects.

left This strung low chair has tribal origins, indicated by the crudely carved designs. The naïve fabric designs are hand block-printed in indigo by John and Faith Singh. Such old local furniture is often small and light—as in the case of the charpoy bed shown on the opposite page—so it can be easily transported.

opposite The *haveli* has been minimally furnished in order not to detract from the feeling of space.

artwork Geometric designs taken from the chair back. The same designs are used by tribal communities in western Gujarat.

right The building design ensures that the *haveli* remains deliciously cool despite the midday summer sun. The stone floors always remain cool, and they are also very easy to swab down, which is essential in such a dusty climate as this. Brackets, corbels, and the corners of the ceilings in this public room have been painted with delicate floral motifs. The dado has been kept simple with square black outlines that accentuate the proportions of the room.

pratima haveli

Pratima *haveli* is a fine example of a genteel inner-city mansion in the heart of Ahmedabad. When it was built some four centuries ago, the intricate wood carving with which it is decorated was a symbol of the region's industrial wealth. But, like so many others in the warren of narrow lanes and alleys of the old city, the *haveli* had fallen into neglect and disrepair. Saved from an ignominious end at the hands of ruthless property developers and restored by John and Kinnari Panikar with dedication and meticulous care, it has become an inspirational symbol of the successful survival of the inner city.

previous pages: left The main bedroom contains a naïve painting on glass of a local potentate.

previous pages: center Traditionally, bathing involved a simple bucket and a cup placed on a small wooden stool, but this bathroom signals the arrival of the Industrial Age.

previous pages: right The floor covering is a traditional mud surface, but notice the Edwardian-style chandelier and the trompe l'oeil ceiling of cherubs and Scottish Highland stags.

opposite A naïve children's toy: the emerald-green parakeet of India.

above left Most *havelis* have sets of double doors to the outside. The outer doors are used when the occupants are in residence, the grilles allowing air to flow freely. The heavy second set of doors is closed when the house is empty.

above right The dilapidated tiles on the floor were replaced by nineteenth-century Italian tiles.

artwork Taken from one of the tiled floors in a wooden *haveli*.

above A second bedroom in the *haveli* mixes the traditional and foreign—with the deckchair alongside the mattress and bolster pillows ranged in the corner. In the foreground, there is a *hitchkar*, a recurrent Gujarati feature that helps to beat the stifling summer heat. Overheated victims drape themselves over the seat and flick the floor gently with a foot to create a refreshing movement of air as the *hitchkar* gently swings back and forth.

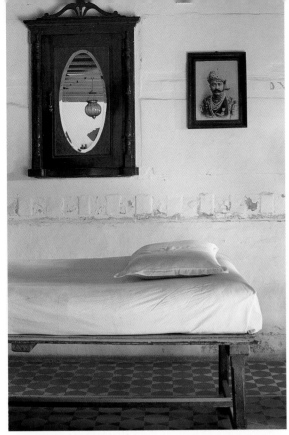

left A simple daybed and pillow for afternoon siestas, covered in traditional white cotton, sits in the first-floor front room. The mirror reflects the serried ranks of wooden beams on the ceiling. The wood came from as far away as Southern India and Burma four hundred years ago. The glass pumpkin lamp is of a type found in many old houses across Rajasthan and Gujarat.

below The kitchen area is part of the dining room. Black granite has been used to create the work surfaces. Brass utensils and storage jars are displayed throughout the kitchen, brass being the most commonly used material for this purpose. On the back wall stands an old samovar for dispensing hot *chai* (tea). A metal basket in which fresh produce can be safely stored out of reach of the ants hangs from the ceiling.

right Interior designer and decorator Raseel Gujral Ansal wanted to revive this Raj-period bungalow by integrating the old along with the contemporary. So the striped fabric on the Edwardian garden furniture is balanced with modern wrought-iron candlesticks. The stripes on the walls are in a shade reminiscent of golden sand made damp by the rain.

opposite Deep colonnaded verandas are the hallmark of the Raj bungalow and would have been used for coffee mornings and tea parties. The *chics* (split bamboo shades) are also typical of the period, essential for keeping the heat at bay while accommodating any favorable breezes.

raj bungalow

Built in the early twentieth century to house the civil servants of the British administration in their grand new capital, New Delhi, bungalows represent an important aspect of the history of Delhi and pre-Independence India. Their construction—thick walls, high vaulted ceilings, and deep verandas—is perfectly suited to the climate, but they were not built to last, and only recently—with many now in a state of disrepair—has realization dawned of their importance as a record of a vanished way of life. Designer Raseel Gujral Ansal of Casa Paradox has illustrated how effectively such an interior can be transformed into a small but sumptuous jewel box, unashamedly celebrating past splendors.

opposite above left The wall-hanging shown here is an exquisite piece of Mughal silk embroidery.

opposite above right Most of the antiques and *objets d'art* are family heirlooms but some are from contemporary European markets such as Portobello in London.

opposite below The drawing room at the center of the bungalow is protected by rooms on all four sides, including the deep verandah, so it is well insulated from temperature extremes.

right The family has an extensive collection of silver heirlooms. A pair of ceremonial silver maces and an ornate, silver throne are shown here. These items are combined with royal family portraits, regal furniture, and *zardozi* (gold- and silver-embroidered velvets) to echo the sumptuous nineteenth century interior decoration.

artwork Detail of a stencil pattern by Raseel Gujral Ansal for the hallway and drawing room.

dehra dun

Dehra Dun, formerly one of the smaller summer retreats of the British Raj, lies in the lower foothills of the Himalayas, surrounded by wooded hills whose summits are frequently shrouded in mist. The interiors of this 1970s house on the outskirts of the town represent a revival of interest in the ephemeral objects of the Raj, harking back to the cluttered comfort of the British country house. Filled by Bikram Grewal with colonial period furniture, and decorated with floral fabrics alongside an extensive collection of botanical paintings, drawings, and lithographs, it illustrates the passion for gardening in a region with one of the highest rainfalls in the world.

opposite left Until recently an open veranda and now used for afternoon siestas, the space referred to as the "sulking room" captures the warm watery light on fall afternoons. The rocking chair dates from the 1940s and consists of single strips of wood shaped by steaming.

opposite right An early-nineteenth-century print of a courtly scene is featured within the headboard of this elegant Edwardian-period four-poster bed from South India.

left Two Edwardian single beds have been artfully joined together to make a sumptuous double. A botanical theme is evident throughout, reflecting Bikram Grewal's own passion for the garden, as well as for botany and ornithology.

left One of the finds of which Bikram Grewal is most proud is the handsome Burmese trunk with its bulbous pillow feet, spotted by him when dining in a restaurant in Bangalore, South India. When he paid for his food, he also paid for the trunk. The planter's chair is well adapted to a warm climate, as the rattan back does not retain body heat as would a solid, upholstered piece of furniture. In addition, its shape is perfect for afternoon siestas. A fine example of an eighteenth-century Kashmir shawl has been used as a bedspread.

right above and below These bird details are from the mural painted by Alpana Khare, which hides the closets behind and injects an element of Chinoiserie into the room.

modern

| john & faith singh | amit ambalal | jaya wheaton | palam margh |
| mallika sarabhai | munnu kasliwal |

above left Aam Niwas, the home of John and Faith Singh in Anokhi, Jaipur.

above right Amit Ambalal's 1970s house rises dramatically out of the soil, a controversial building in its day.

opposite A mosaic illustration of a Cyras crane, a bird that migrates through Gujarat from central Asia. They are a common sight in the fields in winter around Mallika Sārabhai's country retreat.

artwork on page 122 Design taken from a contemporary painting of lotus flowers from Nathdvara, Rajasthan.

The modern Indian house, particularly those built for the urban elite, reflects India's willingness to mix cosmopolitan influences with its own traditions of design and decoration. Two of the houses here represent pure internationalism. Amit Ambalal's 1970s modernist structure by French architect Bernard Kohn was ambitiously experimental for its time, using a combination of cement, iron, and wood that had rarely been tried before in India. Raseel Gujral Ansal's project in New Delhi, by contrast, was for clients from the Shekhavati region who wanted to follow the tradition of building a grand *haveli* to reflect their business success.

The homes of John and Faith Singh near Jaipur and Mallika Sarabhai outside Ahmedabad share an awareness of the great ecological value of traditional indigenous building methods using only local materials. A desire to escape from India's overwhelmingly frenetic and congested urban sprawls has encouraged the popularity of the house on the farm, essentially a country retreat secluded in its own grounds. Two such examples here are both from Jaipur. They are Munnu Kasliwal's recently built small country house, and Jaya Wheaton's family home built in the 1950s, a time when environmental issues and the decline of traditional skills were of little interest to builders and architects.

John and Faith Singh's farmhouse is their permanent home throughout the year. Their aim was to merge the interior and the exterior, setting ponds, courtyards, and verandas at the heart of the building. As with their *haveli* at Amber, the entire project was to be carried out using traditional materials, technologies, and skills.

The land had been used for growing wheat until John planted groves of mango trees. When building began in the late 1980s, the plan of the house evolved partly to avoid any uprooting of the trees. Faith imposed her own special emphasis, wanting to make the most of the Indian sunlight that sends golden shafts through the house at sunrise and sunset. When the sun is higher and hotter, it is filtered by intricately pierced stone *jalis* (screens). Skillfully positioned lily ponds also reflect light inward, creating soothing rippling effects on walls and ceilings. Throughout the house, stained-glass motifs set high in the walls in traditional patterns, throw subtly changing, multicolored patterns onto the floors and walls.

It is hard to believe that the house once stood in a wilderness. Over the past fifty years, the city has expanded to engulf the Wheaton house and extend far beyond it, and the building now stands like an island representing a more

bucolic way of life. Amit Ambalal's house in Ahmedabad, also originally built in a rural setting, is now similarly embraced by urban sprawl.

Born into one of the great cotton-baron families of Ahmedabad, Amit Ambalal has continued the tradition of forward-looking liberalism that has distinguished the city's industrialists over the centuries. He demonstrated his spirit of experimentation and his faith in the future by employing the modernist architect Bernard Kohn to design a new family home for him in the 1970s. The initial premise for the project was again the need to escape the city, but it was also part of an explicit internationalism, itself part of the psychology of post-Independence India. Ambalal, himself one of India's most celebrated post-Independence painters, is influenced in his work by the Russian literary giants Chekhov and Turgenev.

The building caused a huge stir in the city that is home to India's most distinguished school of architecture and design. Why did he choose a foreign architect? Bernard Kohn had thrown down the gauntlet. If Ambalal had the courage, he could design a contemporary space for him in a modular form that would both meet all his needs and, most important of all, be sensitive to the strong Indian

tradition of the extended family. Ignoring all criticism, Ambalal took up the challenge.

The interior of the house is dominated by works of art. Ambalal developed a passion for collecting at an early age, and now has many magnificent pieces of stone statuary and bronze, as well as the finest and most comprehensive collection of Nathdvara paintings in the world. In 1986, he built a studio in the garden as a private space for his own painting, using materials from a four-hundred-year-old *haveli* that had been knocked down in the city.

The Wheaton house was built as a modern bungalow arranged according to traditional principles. There was a large open courtyard exposed to the sky, the center of family life, and a social area in which the cooking was done. In the 1980s, Jaya Wheaton added a second story to be used as her art studio, and modernized the building to incorporate domestic changes and Western influences, including a refrigerator, a cooking stove, and a dining-room table. Today, the interior is dominated by her own paintings, depicting traditional images and people of Rajasthan. These pictures complement her own extensive collection of textiles and antiques, the colors and textures of which in turn provide inspiration for her art. She also collects tribal

above left An antique carriage in the carport of Amit Ambalal's home. The old wooden structure contrasts with the minimalist concrete design of the building.

above right The living room of artist Jaya Rastogi Wheaton, dominated by her paintings based on rural images of Rajasthan.

silver jewelry and everyday objects such as brass *thali*s and *katori*s (eating trays and bowls), loving the simplicity of their shape and the techniques used in their manufacture.

Other projects are more extrovert and cosmopolitan. Casa Paradox, run by Raseel Gujral Ansal with her husband and business partner, Navin Ansal, challenges the Western-inspired "shabby chic" trend ("We are tired of shabby chic, we're surrounded by it!") with an urban internationalism that is fostering the development of a distinctly Indian post-Independence language of design and decoration. Favoring the assimilation of cosmopolitan ideas without rejecting Indian roots, it is a movement that can be seen at work in their latest project in Delhi for a leading Marwari businessman.

This grand Delhi town house illustrates perfectly the continuation of the traditional "showcase" culture of the Marwari business community, adapted to suit early–twenty-first-century aspirations, practical needs, and comforts. The interior was designed as a free-flowing series of spaces, with furnishings and designs referring subtly back to the Art Deco style. It is certainly not cluttered, but comfortable, contemporary, and chic.

Mallika Sarabhai's isolated farm retreat is rigorously minimalist in concept and function—a place for meditation and the enjoyment of nature—but it also had to be a comfortable, practical space that she could share with her two children and four dogs. As one of India's most distinguished classical dancers with her own troupe, as well as being a media executive and spirited campaigner for causes including women's rights and environmental issues, Sarabhai urgently needed the privacy her refuge provides.

Absolute simplicity was the keynote from the start. The house was to be as discreet as possible and completed on a restricted budget. Minimal plans were drawn up following the precepts of Vastu Shastra, an ancient Hindu belief system that aligns the inner self with the outer environment, in some respects resembling *feng shui*. Adobe was used on the exterior walls, not only for its esthetic qualities and because it integrates well, but also because it acts as a natural insulation material. The circular indentations made with a *vatki* (steel bowl) create shadows, so that only half the wall surface is in direct sunlight at any one time.

A sunken courtyard is left open to the sky, thus creating a funneling effect that helps keep the house cool and also acts as a seating area when dry or a paddling pool

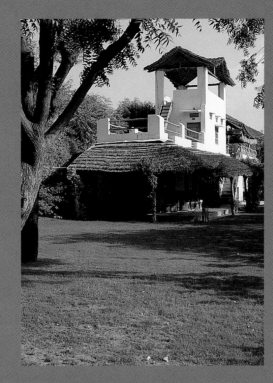

for the children when it is filled with water. In the evening, Sarabhai often floats flower petals and candles on the water, for decorative effect.

In complete contrast to Ambalal's modernity is Munnu Kasliwal's farmhouse near Jaipur, designed to induce a sense of gentle tranquillity in the face of India's headlong and enthusiastic rush to meet the challenges of the twenty-first century, and indeed the hectic pace of Munnu's own jet-set lifestyle. Joint owner, with his two brothers, of Gem Palace, one of India's finest and longest-established jewelers, he represents the youthful arm of the family, creating new designs that are causing a stir among connoisseurs in Paris and New York.

A major attraction of the site was its position among the Aravalli hills, providing dramatic views in one direction of the great fortifications of Amber and Jaigarh, and in another, of a secluded hilltop temple. Kasliwal has created three separate terraces along the length of the building, the middle one raised by means of a traditional method of insulation involving earthenware pots and layers of stone slabs. He has kept this veranda uncluttered, with just two quilted *charpoys* that invite you to stretch out and stargaze into the wonderfully clear night sky.

The building is a series of extensions to what was originally just a simple cowshed. Local craftsmen were used on this project at every stage, and all the wood was sourced from trees that were felled around the building, in particular the eucalyptus that has been mistakenly grown *en masse* in India, draining the land of its precious water supplies in the process. These trees were replaced with mango and neem—the latter for its antiseptic properties—alongside orchards of guavas, cherimoyas, and pomegranates. The whole building is focused around outside living, with the surrounding garden—planted with jacaranda, acacia, morning glory, and jasmine—flowing freely around the house.

As well as restoring the historic Chanwar Palki Walon-Ki *haveli* in Amber, Nimish Patel and Parul Zaveri of Abhikram, Ahmedabad, also work on contemporary projects that are distinguished by their use of traditional design and building concepts. Their professional aim has always remained focused on respect for ecology and tradition, but in contemporary homes such as those they have built for Mallika Sarabhai in Gujarat and John and Faith Singh in Jaipur, they have made a point of including some intriguing additional features.

above left The impressions in the mud wall of Mallika Sarabhai's home ensure that part of it is always in shadow, helping to keep the building cool.
above center Munnu Kasliwal's country retreat outside Jaipur has roof terraces at different levels.
above right Simplicity is the key for Kasliwal, with furniture of wood, locally made wrought iron, and plain cotton fabrics.

john & faith singh

The family house near Jaipur of John and Faith Singh, of the hand block-printing company Anokhi, shelters among mango groves planted and painstakingly cultivated by John. The house illustrates just how effectively local materials and traditional technologies can be adapted to a contemporary context, coexisting successfully with the immediate surroundings and climate. Taking advantage of the brilliant Indian light was of prime importance to Faith, who also wanted spaces linked with free-flowing ease. John, a passionate gardener, was keen to create a harmony between the interior and the exterior through an outward-looking design that keeps the profusely planted garden always visible.

opposite Faith Singh creates a collage of design and color imposed over an interior painted in white limewash and distemper. The bolster pillows shown are inspired by tribal needlework.

below left The new house perpetuates the tradition of the enclosed courtyard, but there are plenty of openings to the gardens beyond.

below right The courtyard contains a marble fountain. whose design was commissioned by the Singhs. Deftly mixing old and new, the latter is represented by the beautifully carved pierced stone *jalis* (screens).

artwork Reproduction of an old hand block-print, Rajasthan.

amit ambalal

Leading contemporary artist Amit Ambalal's 1970s home in Ahmedabad has broken all the usual rules of Indian building. Designed by the French architect Bernard Kohn, it features a modular construction in cement, iron, and wood that was revolutionary in both building materials and techniques. Today it provides a backdrop to Ambalal's remarkable collection of Indian art and sculpture, particularly his series of Nathdvara paintings of the blue god, Lord Krishna, considered the finest in the world. Parts of an old wooden *haveli* have been adapted to create his painter's studio, thus bringing together the oldest and the newest of styles in one place.

opposite left The huge wood-paneled, pivoted door leads into the concrete portico and the garden. The rigor of the concrete finish is tempered by terracotta pots and abundant greenery.

opposite right Detail of the small inner courtyard in the dining area. The courtyard provides essential light and circulation in this room at the heart of the house.

below The dining arrangements are Western in influence, diners are seated at a high dining table, as opposed to sitting on the ground, Indian style. The manner of eating is traditionally Indian; the food is served in *thali*s and eaten mainly with the hands. On the left, there is a Gujarati brass dowry chest on a stand and on the right, an old black-and-white photograph of Indian princes.

above left The chair by Axel Horn adapts a traditional bolster pillow to form the back of the chair. On the wall is one of Amit's Nathdvara paintings of the blue god Lord Krishna. The stone statue on the left is of the sun god Surya.

above right An old silver-plated temple stool supporting a temple tray is the focal point of the room. Above is a modern rug in blue, the color of Lord Krishna. The rug below it is in the traditional Persian/Mughal style.

opposite The communal room shows Ambalal's varied tastes. In the foreground, there is a traditional Indian *charpoy*; while Western-style armchairs line the back wall.

artwork Monochrome rendition of a Nathdvara painting showing lotus blooms and leaves.

opposite A contemporary piece of metal folk art, featuring the figures of a monkey and a peacock.
right Ambalal has built a studio in which to paint. Situated in the garden, it stands away from the main building and provides a tailor-made space for his creative work. The wooden fabric of the building is decorated with intricate seventeenth-century wood carvings that were taken from a *haveli* in the old city which had been demolished.
artwork Detail from the intricate, wood-carved façade of Amit Ambalal's studio.

jaya wheaton

This family home was built outside Jaipur in the 1950s by Jaya Wheaton's father as an escape from the busy city. Modernized in the 1980s, with the addition of another floor to serve as an art studio space for Jaya Wheaton, it is an intriguing mixture of old Indian tradition, new Indian ideas, and Western influence. The artworks displayed on the walls present Wheaton's distinctive romantic interpretations of Rajasthani traditional life, and are complemented by her extensive collection of exquisite village and tribal textiles, acquired during numerous sketching trips into the desert. The paintings and textiles both contrast with the contemporary furniture made by her son, Samir Wheaton, one of India's leading designers.

opposite An outside seating area at Jaya Wheaton's home. Her collection of textiles displayed in the house was acquired through Jaipur cloth markets and trips to the villages and country fairs.

left Wheaton's paintings have a distinctive, figurative style inspired by rural life and tribal communities. Texture is integral to her work, with marble and zinc powder and smashed witch balls for the mirror work, which is also a traditional effect frequently used in interior decoration.

below Many areas of the house include pieces by Jaya Wheaton's son, Samir Wheaton, one of India's leading furniture designers. The low table was designed by Samir and the chair was made for interior decorator and designer Ashley Hicks.

right The spacious quality of the building is accentuated by the free-flowing design. Walls and partitions have been removed and the maximum amount of light introduced. The grand staircase uses a glass balustrade rather than a solid rail, and features an Art Deco curve in the metal supports. The risers of the stairs are finished in black marble and decorated with the Celtic design of linked spirals.

opposite left Raseel Gujral Ansal and Navin Ansal created a contemporary classic interior dominated by the gently fluid curves of the Art Deco period.

opposite right A pair of giant, organically shaped vases stand on a deep window ledge against a massive windowpane etched with random spirals, a motif that Raseel likens to fingerprints.

palam margh

This New Delhi home represents India at its most outward-looking. The house belongs to a family whose ancestors came from the Shekhavati district in Rajasthan and who have an impressive pedigree in business. As the grand *haveli*s of that district reflected success in the past, so does this modern home. Raseel Gujral Ansal and her partner Navin Ansal of Casa Paradox have created an interior that is both cosmopolitan and chic, using the traditions of Indian craftsmanship to produce a thoroughly contemporary feel, which complements some outstanding European hand-blown glass and paintings by leading Indian contemporary artist Satish Gujral.

opposite A console table continues the Art Deco theme with a chrome finish and soft curves, topped with black granite from southern India. The glass vases echo the pastel colors in the painting by Satish Gujral, one of India's leading contemporary artists.
far left The rounded form of the sofas and side tables in the drawing room are accentuated by the economic use of dark wood and fabric. The conservative use of the strong Greek key pattern provides dramatic highlights.
left The precise intaglio work in the black granite tabletop was undertaken by stonemasons from Agra.
artwork Detail of the Greek key and olive leaf intaglio pattern from the dining-room table.

above left The walls of the entrance hall are finished in a subtle cream, which creates a dramatic counterpoint for the black marble set in the floor. A black granite tabletop is supported by a discreet iron stand, designed not to obscure the intaglio beneath. Another foreign symbol, the Celtic motif has been adopted here, in the candlesticks, glassware, and furniture.

above right Tantric spirals were introduced into the surface of the sideboard, a cross-cultural echo of the Celtic spiral. The shallow glass bowl with floating gerberas is a familiar sight in the Indian home.

opposite The juxtaposition of color and tone has been used throughout to emphasize the shapes of objects and accessories: the matte-black finish of the softly shaped cat against a pale background; the clean elegant line of the chrome-finished drawer handles against a dark wood background; the metallic reflective surface of the candlesticks against the pale matt background.

artwork The concentric spirals used in the glass window and sideboard top.

mallika sarabhai

Mallika Sarabhai's recently built farmhouse retreat near Ahmedabad was conceived with the tender side of human nature in mind. As she is an inveterate campaigner on environmental issues, most of the house was made from recycled materials, while its energy requirements are provided by solar panels. Intended as a refuge from her demanding work as a dancer, publisher, and media executive, it was built on a restricted budget as proof that an environmentally friendly house was both possible and affordable. It was also designed to have as little impact as possible on its surroundings, and so incorporates traditional tiling and mud finishes on the outer walls.

left There are windows everywhere, to admit currents of cooling air and heighten the enjoyment of the surrounding countryside, birdsong, and garden scents. All the floors consist of simple, polished cement that is colored with dyes. The quilted bed cover was commissioned in Ahmedabad, and the hand-woven rug was made in tribal Kutch.

below left Pillows on the bed, covered in typical embroidery and mirrorwork, are from Kutch in western Gujarat. The pastoral oil painting by Bharati Kapadia echoes the rural setting of the house.

below right There is a consistently cool quality to this interior. White is used throughout and there is a pond in the main living area. The roof is made of wood; metal fixings would have been faster and less expensive to install but they would have radiated heat.

left and below The *hitchkar,* or porch swing, is found in every Gujarati household. This example has an Art Deco-inspired design, evident in the back struts of the seat and the inset ceramic tiles. The *hitchkar* can be located either inside or outside the home, hangs on the veranda, in this case. It can be turned to face either the house or the garden and fields beyond.

opposite Heavy-duty chains are used to hang the *hitchkar.* Here, the brass has been cast with decorative figures and birds.

munnu kasliwal

Munnu Kasliwal has created a sybaritic balm for his hectic lifestyle in country retreat away from the bustle of Jaipur. As one of India's leading jewelry designers, recognized internationally, he has fashioned a space in marked contrast to his jet-setting professional life. Subtly simple, it combines the clever use of natural textiles with naïve furniture made on-site, while the various rooms and terraces effectively bring the interior and exterior closer together. With its many roses and scented jasmine, the garden provides color and perfume throughout the year.

previous pages The interior of Munnu Kasliwal's rustic retreat is unapologetically minimalist. Color and pattern are consciously avoided in the decoration, because Kasliwal feels that these elements can be created in abundance and brought indoors from the garden, also assuring glorious scents. The large flagstones are locally quarried and the low box table is an old writing-desk. Like the low table and stools, this represents the tradition of "floor living" that is still integral to Indian culture.

opposite above left A beautifully woven *charpoy* bed base.

opposite above right A collection of old brass utensils in the kitchen.

opposite below left The only concessions to modernity in the house are electric light, hot water, a refrigerator, and small electric fans. There is no air conditioning and no glass in the windows; simple iron bars replace the latter, giving a constant free flow of air.

opposite below right The brass bathroom sink, beaten out by a local metal smith.

left The natural qualities of wood and stone have a serene, integrated identity in this interior.

previous pages: left The paper star lamp was designed by Tom Dixon for Habitat. All the furniture, doors, and shutters, were made from trees from the surrounding land. Trees such as eucalyptus have been replaced by neem trees whose leaves are soaked to produce a natural insect repellent. **previous pages: right** This beautifully crafted *charpoy*, with lacquered wooden feet, was used by one of the maharajahs of Rajasthan, when he went on *shikhars* (tiger hunts). An antique brass oil lamp in the shape of a parakeet hangs from the ceiling.

opposite left This is the only enclosed room on the second floor. The modern glass candle lamps are used on the roof terraces in the evenings. The shelves are made of stone.

opposite right A butler's tray stands next to an antique copper storage jar, one of a pair, which would have been used for either water or grain.

left In keeping with Indian tradition, Kasliwal has used white and off-white cotton throughout the house and gardens. All the pillows and comforters are designed by Jaipur-based textile designer Gito Patni.

below Of the two terraces, one is covered, while the other is open to the sky and stars at night. Both areas provide bamboo basket chairs that are locally made and finished in white cotton edging. The covered terrace is used during the day and provides useful shade from the sun. The roof is made of grass thatch that is cut locally and bound in a traditional style by local farmers. In winter and on cold evenings, *chics* (split bamboo roller shades) are lowered to enclose the space, while the braziers ensure a congenial atmosphere.

sources

ARTS AND CRAFTS

**Akar Handicrafts &
  Furnishings**
186121/2 & 18618 Pioneer
  Boulevard
Artesia, CA 90701
Tel: (562) 924-3400

Nomad Trading Company
P.O. Box 182
Ambler, PA 19002
E-mail: nomadtrading
  @hotmail.com

**CARPETS, FURNITURE,
ACCESSIORIES**
ABC Carpet & Home
888 Broadway
New York, NY 10003
Tel: (212) 473-3000

**COMFORTERS, EMBROIDERY,
THROW PILLOWS**
Delta Promotions
14 Coventry Court
Fredericksburg, VA 22405
E-mail:lampman @lbigred.com

FURNITURE
Hult Interior Design
594 N. Kennedy Drive
Kankakee, IL 60901
Tel: (815) 932-7611
Fax: (815) 932-8241
E-mail: info@ hultintdes.com

GLASSWARE, BRASSWARE
Exquous Custom Creation
7112 Butler Street
Pittsburgh, PA 15206
Tel: (412) 441-2838
Fax: (412) 621-5549

HANDMADE QUILTS
Designers Delight
6104 W. Highway 377
Tolar, TX 76476
Tel:(254) 835-4137
Fax: (254) 834-3740

**TEXTILES, HOME
FURNISHINGS AND
FABRICS**
California Fashion House
1142 S. Los Angeles Street
Los Angeles, CA 90015
E-mail: noureldine @aol.com

Global Impex, Inc.
844 Sixth Avenue, Suite 409
New York, NY10001
Tel: (212) 684-7714
Fax: (212) 684-7858

Kinnu, Inc.
43 Spring Street
New York, NY 10012
Tel: (212) 334-4775

INDIAN REFERENCES
Abhikram Architects
15 Laxmi Nivas
Paladi 380 007
Ahmedabad
Gujarat
Tel: (91 79) 658 8018

Anokhi
2 Tilak Marg
C-Scheme
Jaipur 302 005
Rajasthan
Tel: (91 141) 750 860

Devi Garh Palace Hotel
PO Box No 144
Udaipur 313 001
Rajasthan
Tel: (91 29) 538 9211
www.deviresorts.com.

Gem Palace
Mirza Ismail Road
Jaipur 302 001
Rajasthan
Tel: (91 141) 374 175

Raseel Gujral Ansal
Casa Paradox Puc. Ltd.
A-574 Lado Sarai
New Delhi 110 030
Tel: (91 11) 696 8591

Neemrana Fort/Palace Hotel
A-1 Hamilton House
Connaught Place
New Delhi 110 011
Tel: (91 11) 335 2233

**Samode Palace Hotel and
  Samode House Hotel**
Gangapole
Jaipur 302 002
Rajasthan
Tel: (91 141) 632 407
reservations@samode.com
www.samode.com

Udai Bilas Palace Hotel
Dungarpur 314 001
Rajasthan
Tel: (91 29) 643 0808
udaibilas@yahoo.com
udaibilaspalace.com

index

author's acknowledgments

Yadavendra Singh, Samode

I owe a huge debt of thanks to all those who introduced me to India and supported and encouraged me from the early days. They are Ramesh and Renu Mathur, Ajmer Alwar and Oman; Meera, Snehal, Ashish, and Aditya Lakhia, Ahmedabad; Suresh and Rashmi Mathur, Ajmer and Dubai; Rear Admiral and Sundri Kapoor and Deepak, Delhi; Scylla Vatcha, Bombay; Sunita and Ajai Kumar, Varanasi; Mr. JN Lal, Ahmedabad; Mr. and Mrs. S. Nair, Ramnagar, Varanasi; Papaji, Rakesh and Papu Tulli, Varanasi; and Lady Meinertzhagen. Thanks must go to those whose generous hospitality and friendship have made this book possible: Rawal Yadavendra and Arpana Singh; Raseel Gujral Ansal and Navin Ansal; Himmat Singh and family; and Bikram Grewal and Alpana Khare.

I would also like to thank the following people for their help, encouragement, and assistance in bringing this book together: John and Faith Singh; Nimish Patel and Parul Zaveri; John and Kinnari Panikar; Maharaj-Kumar Harshvardhan Singh; Archana Kumari; Aman Nath and Francis Wacziarg; Munnu Kasliwal; Amit Ambalal; Jaya Rastogi Wheaton; Himmat Singh and family; Joy and Toy Singh; Lekha and Anupam Poddar; Mallika Sarabhai and The Sarabhai Foundation.

Also thanks to John Snelson for invaluable creative input throughout the project, especially on location, coordinating, and styling, and for his meticulous attention to detail and perseverance with my preparation of the text; Sarah Wicker for her co-ordination and great efficiency; Claire Wrathall who focused the original concept; and my editor Emma Clegg and designer Megan Smith at Conran Octopus for all their hard work, enthusiasm, and creativity.

Henry Wilson is a photographer whose two passions are India and interiors. His work has appeared in many international magazines and newspapers, including *The World of Interiors*, *House & Garden*, *Elle Decoration*, *Architectural Digest*, *National Geographic,* and *Time-Life*. He has undertaken a definitive photographic study of the city for the book *Benares* and photographed Madhur Jaffrey's *A Taste of India.* His photographs have been used as book jackets for works by Anita Desai, Salman Rushdie, and Norman Lewis.